RESTORING HOPE BUILDING FUTURES

A Telling of the Atlanta Youth Academy Story

Dr. Tony Lankford

ISBN: 0692231137
ISBN-13: 978-0-692-23113-5

Foreward

Leroy Barber

First Executive Director of Atlanta Youth Academy
Former President of Mission Year & FCS Ministries
Current Director of Word Made Flesh

Have you ever sat around with people and started dreaming about things, and the questions usually begin with the words "what if?" You know things like what if I could fly or what if we could walk on water? The kinds of dreams that seem so far fetched, while they are nice to think about, they are so outside the realm of reality you quickly move from the moment. It was in 1996 when Donna and I sat in our home in Philadelphia dreaming of a school for urban kids that was done so well we would have to one day limit the numbers of wealthy kids who wanted to attend. The Atlanta Youth Academy (AYA), after nearly two decades, is that place. Our dreams of this place connected with the dreams of Larry Teem. This dream brought us to together in Atlanta and by faith alone AYA now exists. The substance of the hope we could not visibly see at the time is now seen. The story ahead is a powerful one because it shows how faith can move mountains. A story of how urban ministry can achieve the highest of standards when you consider the people you serve to be as special as your own children or family. Many of the struggles that happened along the way were there because the quality was not compromised. This story is one for the ages that shows how God responds when there is faith in action.

The story of AYA is a journey that brought together many people from many places and this convergence of believers seems to have connected with the plan of God for a "time such as this." Everyone who has been associated with AYA, in one way or another, has been changed and inspired. It's that kind of place and that kind of story, one that captures the spirit, ignites dreams and sparks Kingdom imagination (Everyday Missions).

I think the people that have been a part of the AYA story are a testimony to faith, whether it's a parent hoping for a quality education, a donor who believed, a teacher, administrator, or maintenance person. The blending of all these stories is an expression of God that encourages the soul quite deeply.

For ye see your calling, brethren, how that not many wise men after the flesh, not many mighty, not many noble, are called:

[27] *But God hath chosen the foolish things of the world to confound the wise; and God hath chosen the weak things of the world to confound the things, which are mighty;*

[28] *And base things of the world, and things which are despised, hath God chosen, yea, and things which are not, to bring to nought things that are:*

[29] *That no flesh should glory in his presence.*

[30] *But of him are ye in Christ Jesus, who of God is made unto us wisdom, and righteousness, and sanctification, and redemption:*

[31] *That, according as it is written, He that glorieth, let him glory in the Lord.* (1 Cor 1, KJV)

That really is the story when you get down to it. When we were able to believe just enough, and answer a call in our lives; then God showed us exactly what He can do. It still baffles my mind all the miraculous things we saw and continue to see day after day at AYA. God really did take our faith and prove who He was. Unknown people would dare to believe God could do something great right in the middle of Atlanta with little resource (except our faith) and God did it right in our midst. The book of Isaiah refers to a fast that God chooses and if we are true to that fast then God will repair breaches and restore streets for people to live in peace. The hope that continues to be in my spirit is that the young people who enter AYA will one day be the leaders who begin to repair the broken places in our society. They will continue the work begun at AYA This was the hope 16 years ago and remains in our hearts today.

11 And the Lord shall guide thee continually, and satisfy thy soul in drought, and make fat thy bones: and thou shalt be like a watered garden, and like a spring of water, whose waters fail not.

12 And they that shall be of thee shall build the old waste places: thou shalt raise up the foundations of many generations; and thou shalt be called, The repairer of the breach, The restorer of paths to dwell in. (Isa 58, KJV)

I must warn you that engaging this story may be quite challenging to some because you will read a story of how a school has come to be with little earthly resource. The risk involved in reading the AYA story is you may be moved to do something that will seem unwise and foolish. I suppose that would be quite ok with me because the world could use some unwise foolish followers of Jesus fueled solely by faith. My prayer is that many will be pushed to make such gestures. I hope you are moved to believe what God could do in and through you as this story of faith, calling and obedience unfolds on the pages.

I pray that the God of heaven would give you enough strength to leap out into the unknown and then experience the depth of His power.

Contents

1 | TECHWOOD

"Larry, kids from Techwood don't go to college." From the mouth of a typical eighteen year old this may sound like the simple excuse of a young man unwilling to do the hard work of higher education. Long before he founded the Atlanta Youth Academy, Larry Teem would learn the underlying truth of this sentiment when he began working in Atlanta's most infamous housing project, Techwood Homes.

By 1984 when Larry first came to Techwood, Terry Moncrief, one of the fathers of urban missions in the city of Atlanta, had already established a long tradition of ministry in this inner city community. Working with Terry, Larry continued a tradition of using sports to mentor and build community with the children and teens of Techwood. Larry created a basketball league that was successfully run and highly involved in the lives of kids. For many of the kids this was the only way they could play organized ball; after all, Techwood teenagers had a reputation.

Techwood Homes was feared city wide. It was most commonly associated with drugs and sex trafficking. The youth had been labeled by their school and community as trouble, not the kind of kids you would want playing in your recreation or school league. Where others saw conflict and struggle though, Larry saw potential. As far as he could see, basketball, with a good infusion of structure and mentoring, had the power to change lives. After all, it was working for Chuck.

Chuck's grades prevented him from playing for his school's basketball team, but he was very active in the Techwood ministry-led league. And, he was good—so good he received a scholarship to play ball at a junior college. This would have been a great opportunity for any teen but a monumental one for a kid growing up in Techwood Homes.

Chuck was a tough kid, abandoned by his mother, living with his 19 year old sister and basically growing up on the streets. He did not have a lot of successes in life but he loved basketball. Larry remembers the winter day he walked into the gym and proudly announced he had been offered a college scholarship to play ball next year. Everyone celebrated, Chuck had accomplished what many of his teammates dared not dream, he had found a way out.

With the offer on the table, Chuck began talking with the coaches and sifting through the paperwork. For all Larry knew, Chuck was set to start college. Early that Fall Larry ran into him in the neighborhood. "Chuck, why aren't you in school?"

"Larry, I sent them all my paper work but they need my SAT scores. I don't even know what the SAT's are." Chuck replied.

Larry had grown up in a privileged community and attended a private school. Everyone in his class had taken the SAT's in both their junior and senior year. It was standard operating procedure for the upwardly mobile. In his school everyone graduated and it was understood everyone went to college. In Techwood, a different reality of life existed. Chuck was never pushed to take the SAT, in fact he honestly did not even know what they were.

Larry calmed Chuck down and assured him that he would get him SAT tutoring to prepare for the test. Chuck agreed and began a tutoring regimen. For weeks, he attended session after session.

Finally, the last session came, but Chuck did not show up. On the Saturday morning of the SAT, he was nowhere to be found. Back in Techwood, Larry finally tracked the young man down. Confused by what could have possibly kept him from this amazing opportunity, Larry inquired about what had happened. All of Chuck's fears and insecurities came out in one statement Larry went on to hear over and over, "kids from Techwood don't go to college."

Larry continued to operate a growing and impressive sports and camping ministry for inner city youth. Much of the work was made possible through his connection to wealthy suburban churches and individuals with assets they were willing to share with those less fortunate. From a programmatic standard, the ministry progressed in a healthy and vibrant way; kids were off the street and engaged in positive activities, numbers were growing, and the gospel was being preached. In spite of all his accomplishments, Larry recognized a cycle that seemed inescapable.

For the lucky few who were offered a way out, it was not a poverty of resources that seemed to bare the way; it was a poverty of hope. It was a dirty glass ceiling, a cultural norm that inhibited many from rising above their situation. As the years passed Larry would run into Chuck on the streets from time to time. They would exchange pleasantries and Chuck would ask about the basketball league. But nothing in Chuck's life seemed to be heading in a distinct direction. The hard luck story of the legitimate job that never seemed to pan out continues to be his constant refrain.

In the 1980's, Techwood Homes was just one government housing project out of over forty in the city of Atlanta where intelligent, talented young men and women lay hidden in the ruff. Rodney was just such a gem, a bright likable teenager full of potential. If you had met Rodney you would be drawn in by his intense smile and brilliant eyes. In fact, he was given the opportunity to go to a historically African American college in Atlanta with a strong tradition of excellence. At the same time, his magnetic personality helped him secure a job right out of high school that paid several dollars an hour above minimum wage. He was forced to decide, should he go to college and walk in the footsteps of theological, business, and entertainment heroes or take a manual labor job that paid now?

If you're not from inner city poverty, the decision seems simple- delay gratification, become the community hero, go off to school and after graduating make multiple times minimum wage. It's the American dream! For Rodney the decision was shrouded with confusion. He knew college was a big deal, but he had never seen anyone, really known anyone, from his neighborhood or family actually go. We all measure risk and rewards and the cancer that had gained a stronghold in his mind was "your not college material, you will never make it."

College was for a culture full of hope. Rodney was a realist and in his world, *kids from Techwood don't go to college*. As a result, he made the only rational decision he knew. He let go of the dream and made the financially conservative choice. On one hand you applaud Rodney's responsible behavior while on the other hand your heart breaks for the missed opportunity and unrealized potential.

In places like Techwood, the problem with being the best and the brightest is often those with leadership skills are the first to be recruited by gangs and illegitimate businesses. Patch was one of those recruits.

An active part of Larry's ministry, Patch had lost the majority of sight in his right eye during a b-b gun battle as a boy. By teenage years his personality and intelligence secured him a place in a local gang.

A testimony to the power of Larry's ministry, while participating in summer camp he had made a profession of faith, dropped his colors and left the neighborhood gang. One of the traits Larry appreciated most about his relationship with this young man is they would talk "straight up" and Patch would answer any questions asked.

When the "Brady Bill," a national gun control measure, was past to keep weapons out of the hands of criminals, Larry asked Patch his opinion. He laughed and asked Larry if he wanted his Uzi.

"Where did you get and Uz?i" Larry responded.

He said he traded it for a crack rock. Smiling but with a hint of great seriousness, he told Larry, "It's yours if you want it."

Patches' mother, his girlfriend and his children all lived in Techwood. He took his responsibility to provide and protect them seriously. Patch had a felony involving drug trafficking. Larry knew that was serious. In those days you could not even get a job tearing tickets at the nearby Georgia Tech stadium with a felony record. Patch was at a crisis of faith. Seeking advice from Larry one day he explained, "even if I could get a sweat job, I'd be working 40 hard hours a week hauling garbage making barely $200. I can stand out in the breeze way of my apartment complex and make that in twenty minuets selling dope. What am I supposed to do?"

Patch knew what was "right" but he also knew it was his responsibility to provide for his family. It is easy for a person from an upwardly mobile, achievers mind set to quickly pass judgment on Patch. But these types of dilemmas were what made up daily life for those with whom Larry worked. In Techwood, carrying a gun and selling a little dope were cultural norms. Everyone knows you are not supposed to, but no one takes it too serious when it happens.

Patch was a man of great faith; in another life he would have been an impassioned and captivating preacher. But in this life he was caught up in the spiritual, emotional, and at times physical war zone of his streets. Not only was his physical vision impaired, he also struggled to see past the culture norms in which he lived. Larry says there were flashes of spiritual brilliance that were all too quickly washed over by the harsh realities of making a living in the hood.

Why? What happened? Techwood Homes began as a place of promise and hope. Built in 1935 by the city of Atlanta, Techwood Homes was the first urban housing project in the United States. It, along with the many that followed, afforded the poorest in an urban area the opportunity to live in a place with such modern amenities as a bathtub and electric range in every unit. It was thought to be a progressive move on the government's part. Techwood Homes offered families a safe place to transition out of the "slums" hoping that one day these families may experience the pride of home ownership. In fact, Truett Cathy, founder of Chick-fil-a and one of the countries most success business entrepreneurs lived a portion of his life in these same Techwood Homes.

Due to the lack of fair housing laws and the creation of the Interstate system post WWII, many predominately white families fled the city to create and fill sprawling suburban neighborhoods. This left the African American community to fend for themselves in the city. Although not a perfect situation, many urban areas in the U.S., Atlanta included, blossomed with vibrant African American culture. Business leaders, musicians, and ministers were all raised in these inner-city communities. Many of these leaders fought hard for civil rights; some died in an effort to see equality extended to all people. The modern day hero, Martin Luther King Jr., was reared, educated and rose to prominence in one of these vibrant communities of Atlanta.

Finally, after much hard work, a certain level of equality was granted, at least on paper. The establishment of the Fair Housing Act of 1968 meant that persons, regardless of skin color, were free to purchase homes anywhere they wished. This legislation opened the door for African Americans with means to leave the neighborhoods that filled the inner city. Unintentionally, this left a void of leadership in business, skilled labor and education in its wake.

Techwood Homes, as well as many public housing centers, ceased to be a place of transition, but became a place of permanent residency. In response, the government sought to assure public funds were being used to assist only the poorest of the poor. They began to lower the bar of those qualified to stay in public housing developments. Not wanting or having the means to move, families and individuals sought or forced themselves to meet the lowering bar of expectation presented to them by the government. If married couples could not gain access to public housing one resolution would be not to marry, just live together. If being a single mother would bump you up on the list to secure project housing, not a problem. You simply figured out who to survive within a system that promoted a downward life situation.

This is, of course, a sweeping generalization. But it speaks to how Techwood Homes, a place built to alleviate the slums of Atlanta, had degenerated into the cities worst by the time Larry Teem arrived in the 1980's. Even the best and the brightest of its youth had little chance of rising above its cultural expectations. A place where teens were simply living out the self fulfilling prophecy, "kids from Techwood do not go to college."

Like many of those whom Jesus came to heal and release, these young men had trouble seeing a future beyond the present. The message of Jesus, however, creates room for life altering transitions and helps one exchange a survivor mindset for one of expectation and anticipation. In the end, Jesus offers what the world cannot give—hope. And Jesus knew this mentality of low expectation all to well.

The next day Jesus decided to go to Galilee. He found Philip and said to him, 'Follow me.' Now Philip was from Bethsaida, the city of Andrew and Peter. Philip found Nathanael and said to him, 'We have found him about whom Moses in the law and also the prophets wrote, Jesus son of Joseph from Nazareth.' Nathanael said to him, 'Can anything good come out of Nazareth?' Philip said to him, 'Come and see.' John 1:43-46

Early in the gospel of John we are introduced to some of Jesus' disciples. One of these early followers was Philip. After seeing Jesus, he was convinced that Jesus was the Messiah. He ran to find Nathanael in hopes of sharing this good news. Upon Nathanael learning Jesus was from Nazareth, Nathaniel without hindrance responded, "Can anything good come out of Nazareth?"

According to the scriptures, this small town of Nazareth was Jesus' hometown. For most people, their hometown is an important location. It is the place you develop your foundation of beliefs and values. As a child, your hometown is your world and even when you are unaware, you run, play, and learn at the mercy of those who surround you. In many ways, though certainly not all, you live into the expectations presented to you by the culture of the community in which you grow up. Your community shapes you.

According to Nathanael, nothing "good" can come from Nazareth. What did he mean by this word "good"? It was a common word in the Greek world but has some interesting nuances. For example, in the gospel of Matthew, the Greek word for "good" is used to describe those gifts, given to God's children, that are useful and beneficial (Mt 6:8). In the gospel of Luke "good" has a slightly different meaning; it is used to describe fertile and productive soil (Lk 8:8). By understanding these nuances, we can better understand what Nathanael was saying. For Nathanael, not only could nothing good come from Nazareth but nothing productive or beneficial to society could come from Nazareth.

Nathaniel's comment was the equivalent of a modern day racial slur.

Why would anything good come from Nazareth? Nazareth was not a big town. It was a city that paled in comparison to its neighbors. Nearby multicultural towns, such as Tiberias and Sepphoris, were more glamorous and full of opportunity. It was known that Nazareth did not have fertile soil or access to good water, and as a result, sickness and disease were common. It was pretty clear that Nazareth had little more to offer its residents than poverty and it definitely did not offer its residents opportunity. Perhaps Nathanael had good reason to assume nothing good could come from that place.

In Luke 4, Jesus returns to his home of Nazareth. Like all good, God-fearing children he goes to the synagogue where he preaches. There he began to live out and proclaim a powerful, culturally defiant message that one cannot be bound by the expectations of others. He stood, took the Isaiah scroll, and said:

"The Spirit of the Lord is upon me,
because he has anointed me
to proclaim good news to the poor.
He has sent me to proclaim freedom
for the prisoners
and recovery of sight for the blind,

to set the oppressed free,
to proclaim the year of the Lord's favor." 4:18-19

According to Luke 4:22, "All were amazed at the words that came from his mouth." It was about this time that one listener asked, "Is not this Joseph's son?" Immediately after the words left the mouth of this bystander, the mood in the room began to shift.

22 All spoke well of him and were amazed at the gracious came from his lips. "Isn't this Joseph's son?" they asked.

23 Jesus said to them, "Surely you will quote this proverb to me: 'Physician, heal yourself!' And you will tell me, 'Do here in your hometown what we have heard that you did in Capernaum.'"

24 "Truly I tell you," he continued, "no prophet is accepted in his hometown...."

28 All the people in the synagogue were furious when they heard this. 29 They got up, drove him out of the town, and took him to the brow of the hill on which the town was built, in order to throw him off the cliff. Luke 4:22-24, 28-29

Jesus responds to the bystander's question by expressing his knowledge of their desire for him to stay, work and heal in their own midst. Jesus was on a mission to bless all people, not merely the Jews in Nazareth. Apparently the hometown crowd misunderstood Jesus' sermon because they expected Jesus to act like Joseph's son, a kid from Nazareth and nothing more. When Jesus proposed an idea that was larger, more grandiose than their expectations, he was taken out of the city and nearly killed (Luke 4:25).

All of this leads me to believe that perhaps Jesus had heard comments like Nathanael's before—"Nothing good comes from Nazareth." Who knows? Jesus might have heard similar remarks all of his life. Perhaps he was far too aware of this stereotype, of this low cultural expectation for him. We can never know, but one has to wonder how many of Jesus' childhood friends bought and lived into the lie that nothing good can come from Nazareth.

It wasn't just his hometown that Jesus had to overcome. Let one not forget the scandal surrounding his birth. Mary, the mother of Jesus, was pregnant well before she was to be wed. Jesus was born into one of the most shameful situations of his day.

Jesus' culture understood that the actions of your family determined whether you were a person of honor or a person of shame. There were very clear societal rules and vows that you were to adhere to. If you opposed one of those rules it was considered shameful. Giving birth without being wed certainly placed Mary in the shame category. Further, in this early Palestinian culture, honor begat honor and shame begat shame. Why would God use this shameful situation to birth God's own son?

Through his birth, as well as his life, Jesus proclaimed that God does work through and overcomes any and all cultural limitations and expectations that threaten to limit us and keep us from enjoying our victory in Christ. Culture may say that an unwed, pregnant, teenage mother may not amount to anything, but Mary was chosen by God to be an example of God's use of the humble (Luke 1:48). Culture may expect a teenage father to abandon his girl when he hears that she is with child, but God came to Joseph and told him not to be afraid (Matthew 1:20).

God reaches across the expanse of history and continues to surprise us by transforming cultural and societal norms with the gospel message. Society may convince young people like Chuck that kids from Techwood do not go to college. Others may proclaim a message of security and easy wealth in illicit activities. The gospel of Jesus calls everyone to cast those voices and expectations aside in order that they might live fully into their rightful place within God's kingdom work here on the earth.

During the summer of 1996, the world was focused on the Olympic Games that were being hosted in the city of Atlanta. Larry, however, saw another side to the public relations blitz that was taking place. The city leaders had built new venues, cleaned up major tourist corridors, and conveniently shuffled poverty to the side. Millions saw countries from all over the world compete in the progressive, clean, well-prepared capital of the South. Daily Larry experienced a population of residents disinherited from all that this grand city had to offer.

Larry began asking dangerous questions about what it really meant to follow Christ. Year after year Larry saw more kids killed and imprisoned than he did going to college. What does presenting the gospel of Jesus Christ, the message of the Kingdom of God, look like in this kind of situation?

By asking such questions, Larry began to understand that if he, if the body of Christ, was going to affect any change in the lives of these teens then he must create a new culture. He needed an avenue by which these kids would grow up hearing a whole new story, one infused completely with the power and hope of the biblical narrative.

In time Larry became thoroughly convinced nothing creates culture for kids like school. Thus, he made the decision to create one, but not just any school. He envisioned a school that had the ability to come alongside all children, including the disenfranchised students he saw in Techwood Homes and other inner city neighborhoods. He knew it would need to be Christ-centered and on par with the highest academic standards. This dream was the birth of the Atlanta Youth Academy.

The Atlanta Youth Academy is a private Christian school that began by working with children from Techwood Homes. A school that to this day is seeking to be the hands and feet of a culturally defiant Jesus. Many children grow up with the voice of Nathanael swirling all around them. "what good can come from ..." It is no wonder Chuck was scared to go to college. It is easy to comprehend why Rodney would choose work over the investment of higher education. One could even fathom how the lure of dealing drugs was attractive to Patch when there are no other foreseeable options for success.

Obviously, there is no ethical justification for this kind of illegal activity. If, however, the gospel as presented by Christ is truly about alleviating the barriers that keep us from discovering our place and purpose within God's Kingdom work on this earth, then that must affect how we live and act. Jesus presents a Kingdom possibility wherein the expectations of the culture at large are not the expectations of God. There in Techwood Homes Larry Teem began to embrace the reality that working alongside the Jesus of the Bible meant nothing less than doing the hard of work of presenting good news to the poor, the possibility of healing for the sick, and freedom to the captives. Larry set out to create a space where all children could hear and experience the Lord's favor.

Questions for Reflection

What has been your experience with inner city poverty?

Have you ever known anyone you felt simply lived into cultural expectations rather than becoming fully who God may or may not have wanted them to be in this world?

Photo © Atlanta History Center

2 | BUCKHEAD

Larry enjoys telling the story of the elephant at the circus who is led around the ring by a simple, small rope attached to his collar. The elephant was, of course, trained to follow the direction of the ring-master. As a young elephant he was led by a large chain, physically forced into submission. The chain began to represent a response: conditioned hope-lessness. As time passed the chain was replaced by a thick rope and then a small lead. But in his mind the chain and the lead were one and the same. He had been conditioned that there was no hope of escape – why even try. He had the ability to break free but he could no longer envision the truth, a life or an alternative way other than following the ringmaster.

Persons who are materially poor are not the only people who need Jesus' help in order to break free from cultural expectations in order to follow God's path for their lives. Before Larry committed his life to doing ministry in Techwood Homes in the mid 1980's, he was on a different path. Larry was living into cultural expectations of his own.

Larry grew up in the affluent, northside area of Atlanta known as Buckhead. His father was an accomplished businessman and his mother was a loving wife with four children. As a child, he was not told that he was rich; instead, his father referred to their situation in life as "comfortable." His father's description seemed fair as Larry grew up wanting for nothing in his families' five thousand square foot home.

Larry was fortunate enough to have parents who were active Christians, so he was reared and discipled in Buckhead's Second Ponce de Leon Baptist Church. As a boy, he was taught the stories of the Bible in Sunday school, was baptized and grew up attending a youth group that had an abundance of activities. In the midst of it all, he was aware of the blessings affluence provides: a strong nuclear family, private school, friends, cars, parties, college, and of course, opportunity.

Larry's father was successful and wanted the same or better for his children. Although the travel required by his job took him out of the home quite a bit, it displayed for Larry a standard of sacrifice and success that would be expected of him one day. Larry's father earned his undergraduate at Auburn University and his MBA at Harvard. After his military tour in Korea he remained in the Army reserves eventually earning the rank of full Colonel. He was everything one would hope to find in a good citizen and role model.

As for Larry, well, he will admit that he was a poor student. Even so, he managed to make his way through the prestigious Lovett School in Atlanta. Upon graduating from Lovett, he continued his education, as expected, at Auburn University. There he met his wife Lisa. It appeared that everything was falling into place.

Upon graduation the doors opened for Larry to go into ministry. One of the first phone calls he received was from a college ministry that was interested in offering him a staff position. Like most people, he asked about the compensation package.

He was told how part of the job would require raising financial support for the position. Outwardly Larry politely declined but inside he was saying "that is not a real job." He remembers as he hung up the phone thinking "I'll never raise support."

Larry soon found a *real* job—a position selling ads for an up and coming business that was on the forefront of technology and innovation. God, however, would not leave Larry alone. Larry was constantly lost in thought by the memory of summers spent as a camp counselor in downtown Atlanta at a place called Techwood Homes. He had a strong sense that God was calling him to ministry, but he and God had worked out an agreement. He had made it clear to God that it would be better if he first spent time in the business world before going into the ministry world. After all, everyone, including God, surely knew how hard it would be to transition back into the business world if ministry did not work out. God would not want us to do anything crazy.

A certain ruler asked him, "Good teacher, what must I do to inherit eternal life?"

"Why do you call me good?" Jesus answered. "No one is good—except God alone. You know the commandments: 'You shall not commit adultery, you

shall not murder, you shall not steal, you shall not give false testimony, honor your father and mother.'"

"All these I have kept since I was a boy," he said.

When Jesus heard this, he said to him, "You still lack one thing. Sell everything you have and give to the poor, and you will have treasure in heaven. Then come, follow me."

When he heard this, he became very sad, because he was very wealthy. Luke 18:18-23

Even in Jesus day there was certainly an expectation of the wealthy. If we look closely at this passage, we learn that the focus is not only this man's wealth but also his position. Luke describes him as a "rich young ruler." He was in a position of power. He had his youth; he had influence; he had wealth. On top of all that, he seemed to have been an outstanding citizen. He did not cheat, murder, steal, or lie. He had kept all the commandments. He was a great son and everything for which a parent could hope. For all practical purposes, this young man had complete control over his destiny. How foolish would it have been for someone with that much ability, opportunity, and control to drop it all and follow someone else?

After this encounter with the "rich young ruler," Jesus turns to his disciples and explains how hard it is to get into the Kingdom of Heaven. In fact, Jesus explains that it is a near impossibility for the rich. Jesus illustrates the difficulty by painting the picture of a camel trying to get through the eye of a needle. Jesus goes on, though, to explain how much more one is to receive in both this age and the age to come when they give something up to follow him. Sacrifice is never easy. Despite the strength of our faith in God, in the Bible, or God's providence, the challenge is always taking the first step towards letting go.

Larry had more to overcome than simple finances if he was to commit his life to addressing the poverty of a demographic not his own. One cannot deny that racism still permeates Southern culture. Though less overt now, it was a daily reality for Larry in the 1970's and 80's. Those who knew Larry's story and the circumstances of his life would have understood, even expected, a hint of southern-bred racism.

Between Larry's junior and senior year of high school, he typified many teens by maintaining a steady beat of hanging out with friends, lazy poolside days, and church youth group events. Life at home was relatively normal. Mom kept the house going and dad traveled for work. One day normal was disrupted.

Larry left youth group, dropped his girlfriend off and headed home. Nearing the house around 10PM, Larry found it odd the street was full of cars. He walked into the crowded house and was immediately greeted by his pastor. There, looking into his eyes, Dr. Marsh told him his father had died. Larry knew that his father was on a routine trip. He did not know earlier that day in Boston a drunk driver killed his dad.

The normal, predictable, comfortable life Larry had lived was shaken to its very core. As details of the accident surfaced, Larry learned that the person who killed his father was a young, African American man who was driving drunk. Only to add to the pain, he learned this man was driving on a license currently suspended for a previous drunk driving arrest. Larry and his family could hardly handle the emotional load of this event. As a family, they made the decision not to go to Boston for the trial of the man who with a complete and selfish disregard for others took the life of a father, a husband, and a provider.

Losing a member of ones nuclear family at a young age is not something you get over but something you learn to live with. The numbness lasted a year before his emotions begin to reengage. It was tough, but life continued, as it always seems to do.

The summer after this traumatic event Larry decided to get a part-time job in order to have some spending money before he headed to Auburn University for his freshman year. He ended up pumping gas for a station on Roswell Road in North Atlanta, a safe enough part of town.

One day, while managing the station by himself, two African American men in there twenties swiftly approached him. Sensing an uneasiness to the situation, Larry's simple greeting, "How may I help you?"

One of the two young men said, "We'll take it all."

One grabbed the cash container and pulled out a gun. The other brandished a switchblade forcing Larry to the back wall with his hands above his head. Larry imagined in a situation like this he would have a commanding voice and snatch the gun out of the hand of the robber. What he learned as a scared, skinny, white kid from Buckhead was you become very polite and silently oblige.

One of the gentlemen asked for the safe, Larry pointed to it on the ground. Meanwhile the other young man began going through the keys hanging on the wall.

"Where's the key, where's the key?' Asked the man with the gun now pointed at Larry's face. As Larry stumbled to answer, the man with the gun instructed his partner to hit Larry. Larry quickly pointed out the appropriate key.

"Open it!" commanded the young man with the gun. Larry sat down on a chair and attempted to open the safe on the ground.

The gunman forced Larry's head down between his legs as his accomplice emptied the safe and ran to the car.

Before he left, he told Larry to keep his head down. He then proceeded to strike Larry with his fist several times in the back of the head to assure his compliance. Larry sat silent for what seemed like an eternity. He did not look up until all was quiet.

As the police questioned him, Larry gave a thorough description of the incident. The police informed Larry that two young men fitting the profile had robbed several stores in the area killing one clerk.

After the robbery Larry felt uncomfortable in the evenings as the sun started to set and he was alone working at the station. Weeks later, Larry learned that the police believed they had found the two suspects. The men, however, were killed in a shootout before the police could arrest them.

After growing up in a wealthy, white, Southern culture, it would seem to most people that these two events in young man's life—the killing of your father and nearly losing his own life — would only solidify the cultural racism he saw all around. How could a young man, whose own grandfather was a member of the Ku Klux Klan in Alabama, go through all of this and not buy into the stereotypes? Others expected Larry to react with fear, bitterness, even hatred towards those who stole so much from him. What could possibly keep someone from reacting solely out of these experiences?

One of the greatest descriptions I know of God is God as the ingenious alchemist. An alchemist is an old-fashioned pharmacist. He would take various chemicals, many of which were dangerous on their own, and mix them with other chemicals to create a healing solution. In much the same way, God's greatness and the extent of His power is found not in the prevention of bad occurrences but in God's ability to transform our lives into a healing solution for the world.[i]

Larry saw this come true in his own life. God took what should have been bitterness and rage and placed in Larry's heart a deep, burning passion to work with young, less advantaged African-American children and teens in the city of Atlanta. This feeling was not birthed out of any sense of so called "white guilt" or pity for those with whom he worked. Larry's passionate call to ministry was birthed out of God's ability to transcend cultural expectations and transform Larry's pain into an overwhelming desire to heal and mend that which is broken in this world.

God did not call Larry in spite of his past, God called Larry because of his past. As a young man, Larry eventually realized this deep fire for ministry would not go away. In spite of everything, God's call burned so deep and so strong it forced Larry to do something crazy. One day he walked into his salary paying advertising job and quit in order to follow God's call into full-time vocational ministry. For those living within the kingdoms of this world, this decision makes no sense. This was, however, the type of decision that Jesus put before the "rich young man." Jesus assured his disciples that the right decision had the potential for great blessings in "this age, and the age to come" (Luke 18:30).

In his own words from a few years back, Larry reflects upon that life changing day.

There are lighting rod moments in life, unforgettable memories frozen in time. Some of these moments are cataclysmic events while others may come in less than a faint whisper. Over 22 years ago while I was a sales associate for an Atlanta based company, a manager gathered his team and was giving his weekly pep-talk. He said "The reason I can go out and sell our product is because it works, it helps our customers, and I believe in it 100%." No sooner had the words come out of his mouth than lightning struck. ... I got up from my desk, went over to my sales manager, turned in my resignation and left the building to seek first the Kingdom of God. [ii]

Questions for Reflection

What in your past may cause you to hold stereotypes towards a certain group of people?

Can you describe a time you have felt a tension between what you or others want you to do and what you feel God may be calling you to do?

3 | DREAMERS

Our experiences shape us in profound ways. If we are not careful, our lives are merely more than re-actions to those experiences. Some of us encounter hardships and difficulties that define us for the rest of our days. It does not have to be this way. While it is true that portions of who we are and what we believe are the products of our past. As people of faith, our past should not shackle our future. Our tomorrow should remain open to revision, with hope fueled from God's ordained possibilities.

After all that Larry went through, he could have resorted to a life of bitterness, but instead of letting his experiences define him, he derived motivation from them. He demonstrated the power of forgiveness by pressing forward with bravery and giving his life to becoming a part of the solution. He quit his job, embraced his call into ministry, and headed back to "the hood" in the early-1990's full time. There he began envisioning a school for boys and girls who were so burdened by their present reality that they could not imagine a different future.

Of course, there is a huge gap between one's dream to create such an academy and the actual reality of having students in a classroom. Unsure what the first step should be, Larry began searching Atlanta to see if there were any existing schools doing a similar work of which he had envisioned. He found only one. On the south side of Grant Park, across the street from the U.S. Federal Penitentiary, there stood a private Christian academy. The school had a Presbyterian, African-American pastor who lived in the community serving as its director. In spite of his best efforts the school was struggling. The community that surrounded the school was made up primarily of government-housing apartments. While the children's parents desired an alternative to the local public school, resources were low.

At this time, Larry was fortunate enough to have an intern, Joel Moore, who had a desire to be a teacher. Larry sent Joel over to the school to see if a partnership was possible. It did not take Joel long to realize that the school faced a number of challenges. At one point, the school's power was shut off, and on another occasion, the water as well.

Although there was little organization, Joel discovered a small school staff with good hearts following a compelling mission. Joel gave it his all and taught at this school for two years. Unfortunately, good intentions were not enough to warrant people's continued financial support. What the school really needed was a new vision and energy, but Larry was not able to rally supporters to invest in a school that many had deemed a financial "black hole."

One of the defining characteristics of good leadership is the creation of a clear vision. In most cases, resources will follow vision. Surprisingly, the opposite is not true. Even if you begin with abundant resources, one's dream -a community's dream - will not be realized without a compelling vision. Early in this process, Larry learned the importance of vision, but he also learned that people give to a person, not just a cause. Further, people's giving is often in proportion to the ministry's level of credibility in their eyes. Each of these insights helped create a strong and sustainable foundation for Atlanta Youth Academy.

Before AYA was a reality, Larry was told over and over again that he should start a school. One of the earliest and most profound voices was that of Marcia Standard who had been Larry's elementary principal at the Lovett School. When she visited the school on the south side of Grant Park it led her to inform Larry that she could not in good conscience support the ministry that was being done at this particular school. She declared, nonetheless, if he were to start a new school, she was sure she and others could support it.

One of his first tasks was to put together an advisory board. Larry needed a group of intelligent, faithful people to hear and reflect. After all, even the best ideas can remain on the ground if you do not take the time to share, refine, and develop those ideas with trusted others.

This first board contained educators, administrators, business people, and possible donors. It was here that Larry really began to understand how God did not accidentally birth him into an upper class Buckhead family. In God's infinite wisdom Larry was positioned exactly where he needed to be to accomplish this seemingly impossible task of starting a school of the highest quality while working with families that could never afford it. Often an organization will only rise to the level of those willing to invest their time, energy, and money. Thankfully, Larry knew great people. Thus, success for this new school began by gathering a group of competent, invested people of faith to share and support the grand vision of what the Atlanta Youth Academy could become.

With the support of the advisory committee, Larry began his search for someone who would be interested taking on the role of Principal and Executive Director. He approached person after person and told them about the job possibility. In spite of Larry's best efforts, potential candidates turned him down again and again. Like Larry only years before, they continued to inquire about compensation. This was a job that required raising one's own support. A job Larry himself had once described as "not a real job."

During the Christmas break of 1996, with the Executive Director job in the back of his mind, Larry headed to Champagne, Illinois to attend the Intervarsity *Urbana* conference. Larry set up a table to promote and recruit for his growing ministry that began in Techwood Homes, a ministry by that time called the Atlanta Youth Project. There he was consistently asked if he had a school. Time and again Larry gave the speech that he hoped to one day have a school but as of now, no. He consistently pointed these young men and women over to another table staffed by a young African-American gentleman named Leroy Barber.

Leroy was working with the nationally renowned Philadelphia urban missionary Tony Campolo helping to recruit teachers for Cornerstone Christian Academy. Eventually, Larry talked with Leroy and described his dream of creating a Christian school in Southeast Atlanta. Leroy had already scheduled a recruiting trip to Atlanta. He made plans to drop by and visit Larry while he was there.

After spending a day together, Leroy began to entertain the idea of accepting the Principal/Executive Director position. Larry was honest with Leroy about the challenges and need to raise his own funds. It is a small minority of people who will step out and raise personal support. At this time, it was almost nonexistent for someone in the African-American community. Leroy left Atlanta, returned to Philadelphia, and Larry assumed the conversation was over.

Back in Philadelphia, Leroy proposed this possibility to his wife. After thought and prayer, they discerned God was calling them to move to Atlanta to help make this vision of Atlanta Youth Academy a reality. Leroy called a surprised Larry and agreed to come alongside and get this crazy idea off the ground. With Leroy on board, AYA was no longer a dream—it was quickly becoming a reality.

Finally, in late summer 1997, two weeks prior to the start of school, Leroy Barber and his family moved to Atlanta and began preparing for the Academy's first year. Nine students from Techwood Homes and one teacher were recruited. With a budget of forty thousand dollars, they met in the basement of Glencastle, a civil war era debtors prison in Grant Park that had been restored by Bob Lupton, founder of FCS Urban Ministries. Years before, Glencastle had been filled with prisoners bound by their circumstances, but with the start of AYA, the once blacksmith shop at Glencastle became a space of redemption, hope, and opportunity.

In AYA's second year, it doubled in size to 18 students. There were definite signs that momentum was building and consequentially, AYA's credibility was growing. Some would say AYA's beginnings were modest, but as Jesus describes more often than not, this is how things of worth in God's Kingdom begin.

He (Jesus) also said, "With what can we compare the kingdom of God, or what parable will we use for it? It is like a mustard seed, which, when sown upon the ground, is the smallest of all the seeds on earth;

yet when it is sown it grows up and becomes the greatest of all shrubs, and puts forth large branches, so that the birds of the air can make nests in its shade." Mark 4:30-32

The parable of the mustard seed is found in each of the synoptic gospels (Matthew Mark, and Luke). In Mark, however, this particular parable is found in the midst of several parables, which each teaching that the kingdom of God is a new reality that functions differently than the kingdoms of this world.

Jesus' audience would have been familiar with mustard seeds and mustard plants. Some of his listeners may have actually viewed mustard plants as a nuisance because they would sprout up anywhere and had the ability to take over an area, which is surprising considering the size of a mustard seed. Though these mustard plants were a nuisance for some with a singular focus, birds of the air found needed shade and security to nest in its branches.

Beginning with only nine students and one teacher, AYA is the product of a mustard seed mentality. It began small and was able to sustain itself because it was tended by individuals who believed God could work through them to impact their community. They believed that God could take something meager and transform it into something meaningful. They believed that with a few people of faith God could turn the insignificant into something magnificent. The world may only see a mustard seed, but faith allows and instructs us to see more.

As the school grew, so did the network of willing donors and supporters. Larry and Leroy were delighted to meet one day with several potential donors who invited them to lunch at the Capitol City Club, one of the most exclusive private clubs in Atlanta. For someone who spends most of their time serving alongside persons with profound need, restaurants like Capitol City Club can be a jarring experience. It certainly was for Leroy.

Larry grew up within the opulence Atlanta can provide, but for Leroy this lunch was a new world. His eyes opened to this reality as he walked through the wooden doors into the heart of Atlanta business prominence. Here at this lunch, Larry and Leroy sat around a white linen table with some of Atlanta's most intelligent and influential people. Unbeknownst to Larry, Leroy doubted how much further he could take the Academy. His heart was in it, but when it came to fundraising at this level, his confidence and sense of call wavered.

Eventually, Leroy decided to step down. It was not an easy decision but one he made in the best interest of AYA. He knew with confidence God called him to start AYA, and with that same confidence he knew he had accomplished what God called him to do. It was now time to step aside and let someone else carry the academy to the next level.

Although Leroy is no longer AYA's Executive Director, he is still a member of its board of directors and offers ongoing support. Currently, Leroy is president of Mission Year, a year-long urban ministry program focused on Christian discipleship and service. It is obvious that Leroy is a leader, and in many ways, AYA is indebted to him for without his commitment to entrepreneurial vision and leadership AYA may have never existed.

Once again though Larry had a school with no leader. This transition plunged Larry and the board into a time of discernment and significant anxiety. How do we afford someone to take us to the next level? How do we continue? If we continue, what kind of leader do we need?

Questions for Reflection

Is there anything you have always dreamed of doing to make this world a better place but have never done? What?

If you were going to make a major life transition, what do you think that would like look? Dream about how you would make that a possibility.

4 | CHUCK

With the loss of its founding executive director, the Atlanta Youth Academy embarked on what turned out to be a multi-year search for the right person to lead the school. Educationally, the school needed someone who understood the dynamics of the k-8 academic system and could inspire teachers to give their best. Practically, the board was looking for someone who had a heart for children and under-served families but also felt at ease with Atlanta's captains of industry, country club set and its most generous philanthropist.

With the school year almost amongst them, in an effort to fill the leadership void, they quickly hired a director who had experience leading a small non-profit. On paper, he had the credentials and was a man of faith. But in Larry's words he was AYA's "Saul." He looked the part, was capable, and when they surveyed the land for a leader he stood head and shoulders above the rest. But the hire was inspired more to emulate the structure of other schools rather than to live by faith. After serving one school year, he did not work out. Frustrated and discouraged, Larry called the team to do something many us often view as impractical when we are faced with high levels of stress and anxiety ... stop ... pray ... and wait.

In following a missional vision, discouragement and doubt are always tapping at the door vying to gain entrance. God had called and equipped Larry and others to develop Atlanta Youth Academy. It was serving an important role in Atlanta, and more importantly, they believed it served an important role within God's Kingdom work. They were seeing great success. Even during the year of transition, AYA's enrollment and funding continued to double. Confident God was involved in this project, Larry and his team continued to trust God and believed God would raise up a leader to shepherd the school and guide it into the future God had planned for it. They started the next school year with no executive director. The executive committee of the board of directors handled the day-to-day operations as they waited.

Larry remembers it like yesterday; he sat down and made a list of what they were praying for in the candidate's experience, heart and capabilities. As he made the list, he used his friend Chuck Johnston as his bench mark. At that time, Chuck was president of the prestigious Whitefield Academy in Atlanta. Not that they dared hope for Chuck, because Larry knew someone of his professional standing was unobtainable for a struggling start-up institution like AYA. Chuck simply personified the ideals they sought in a leader.

Unsure what to do next, the board continued to employ their atypical strategy. They prayed for discernment and patiently waited for God to work. They held out hope that God would raise up a leader like Chuck Johnston to fill this important role.

We probably are not starting a school, but we too encounter roadblocks. We find ourselves in difficult and stressful situations. Instead of employing our faith, we more often than not, find ourselves shackled by our circumstances. We say we want and even seek God's will for our lives, but when the going gets tough, our actions sometimes expose the shallow well of our faith.

An important question must always be asked regardless of our circumstances, what are we actively doing to discern God's will? Are we praying and listening? Are we reading scripture and reflecting? Are we worshipping and experiencing the Holy? Do we ever take the time to sit in silence? If we are honest with ourselves, the answer is most likely no. Yet, we continue to wonder why it seems we are coming up with less than what God would hope or desire for us. When we pray, however, we open ourselves up to God, and we posture ourselves in such a way that we are then able to receive God's wisdom.

It was after taking some time to pray and reflect that Larry's mindset began to shift. For months, they had been looking for someone *like* Chuck Johnston—what if they were to actually ask Chuck Johnston to be the executive director? Such a thought prompted several questions. Why would someone with his education (an impressive combination of Emory and Vanderbilt Universities) lead such a small school? How would finances for such a commanding leader work out? Would he even be willing to leave a school with an abundance of support and staff in order to serve at AYA? Despite the obvious hurdles, Larry became more and more convinced Chuck was the person God had molded and raised up for this very time and situation. But, it was still to be determined whether Chuck felt the same way and would discern such a call.

The Board of Directors had created a separate foundation to raise necessary scholarships for the school. To Larry's great fortune, Chuck Johnston had just been invited to come on as the newest trustee of the foundation board. Frank Briggs the president of the foundation board and close friend of Chuck asked him if he would be willing to have coffee with Larry and talk though some of the leadership issues the school had been facing. Chuck agreed, and Larry met at a coffee shop appropriately named *Sacred Grounds*.

As the conversation ensued, Larry felt that now was the appropriate time to lay it all out on the table. Turning to Chuck, Larry asked, "What would it take for you to come run AYA?"

Chuck first responds with a quick, quiet, but polite laugh. It was the same type of laugh Larry had given years earlier when he was asked to make great sacrifices for the sake of ministry. And, it was the same laugh that earlier candidates for the director position had given Larry when he was starting the school. Chuck respected Larry enough to follow his laughter with the cordial, "I will pray about it."

Most of us say that we will pray about something, but we never do. Chuck actually went home and prayed about it and so did his wife. At this point, Chuck was approaching sixty years of age, and he had an important question to ask himself. Did God have something more for him to do with the last years of his vocational career?

Chuck was no stranger to the inner city. As president of Whitefield Academy, he often took groups of students into the city to volunteer at ministries, including Atlanta Youth Academy. Prior to taking the lead at Whitefield, he oversaw the development of a million dollar scholarship fund that opened up opportunities for students from lower income families to attend prominent private schools around the city. Instead of thinking of how his background and experience may over-qualify him for running a small urban school, Chuck began to wonder if his experience and education had prepared him for such a time and place as this.

Larry was surprised when Chuck called and asked if they could get together and talk through some details. At this meeting, Chuck presented Larry with a list of concerns, which he insisted should be addressed if he were to consider the position. First, he wanted teachers to be paid a more competitive salary. Second, he had a strong conviction, supported by research, that students in lower income demographics experience more academic atrophy during the summer than the average student. Thus, he wanted to extend the school year to 200 days and spread it out over eleven months. He also felt the academy needed to start at K-4 in order to build an early academic foundation. Further, he believed it was important to maintain small class sizes and added that doing so would be essential to the school's continued success.

Chuck's concerns were warranted, constructive, and they displayed his commitment to the institution of education, as well as his concern for educators, students, and academic excellence. More than anything else, his list of concerns was birthed out of his conviction that Christian education must be balanced. Too often, the "Christian" in "Christian education" is emphasized over and above "education." Chuck strongly believed in the importance of faith education and held firmly to the belief that the gospel should be at the heart of the school's belief and praxis. Chuck believed quality academics, done in an affirming environment, by compensated and competent teachers are essentials for success.

All that Chuck proposed completely resonated with Larry. From day one, Larry envisioned a school that had Christ at its center and sought to excel academically to the highest standards. After establishing that they were on the same page, Larry informed Chuck the real issue at this point in their development was not vision but capacity. The school was running low on money, people, and space.

Strangely, this was good news for Chuck. He had experience in several of the most well-known private schools in the state and had served as executive director for the Atlanta Ballet. With these experiences in his back pocket, Chuck knew he could overcome nearly any logistical challenges the school faced.

Just eighteen months from retirement, he decided to leave a high profile, prestigious, successful private school on the north side of Atlanta that he had developed from the ground up and take the reigns of a small school that was struggling to make it in the inner city. In the world's eyes, this decision made no sense: less money, less time, less staff, and less security. But, the way of the Kingdom is backward. The way of descent can lead to greater reward, greater satisfaction, and greater meaning.

"There is a time for everything, and a season for every activity under heaven...

What does the worker gain from his toil? I have seen the burden God has laid on men. He has made everything beautiful in its time He has also set eternity in the hearts of men; yet they cannot fathom what God has done from beginning to end." Ecclesiastes 3:1, 9-11

Seasons of our life do not seem to transition with the ease we often see in the beauty of nature. One minute we are enjoying the warmth of the sun, and before we know it, we are watching snowfall outside our window. Time has passed. We were a part of the process, but somehow missed the transition. Outside the realm of nature, however, transitions are often disjointed and full of the challenge to discern when and where God is calling.

Occasionally, tragedy forces us out into the intersection of life without much warning. Rarely, windfall blesses us with the ability to weigh the hosts of positive options. More often we find ourselves somewhere in the middle where there is a cacophony of voices espousing their opinions. If we are blessed, however, we sense a divine push in one way or the other.

Chuck's decision to take the reigns of Atlanta Youth Academy seemed to go against the flow of cultural expectations or norms. After all, he had achieved a great deal at Whitefield. Whitefield was a better place because of Chuck's leadership and ability to develop an educational institution, but there is no doubt that Whitefield also gifted Chuck. He left a more skilled and experienced leader. He brought these gifts with him to AYA. At sixty plus, no one could fault him for one more vocational transition, a major one at that. He could have easily slipped into a position that was established and secure. With such an impressive resume, he could have moved into the corporate world, and with retirement looming, he had every reason to cushion his nest egg. In the end, however, he exchanged those possibilities for a corner office in order to oversee a school that was lacking sufficient money, space, or people.

Upward mobility and the pursuit of success are not bad. In every generation God raises up Godly men and women like Chuck Johnston to lead, guide, and achieve high levels of success. These men and women often steward their success into generous lives that bless, encourage, and benefit others. But, as the author of Ecclesiastes writes with simple elegancy, "There is a time for everything, and a season for every activity under heaven."

Life has a purpose and it is moving in a direction. In many ways, life is like a worship service. When designed well, there is intentionality, flow, and direction to the service. It becomes more than a meeting. It points to God in so many ways. Chuck's career life had its grand musical pieces. He hit a homiletical high note at Whitefield. His life pointed to God in so many ways and times. One could say that his decision to go to AYA was the climax of that service—a time of offering. A time to respond to what God has done; and then give back to God from that which God had so richly blessed.

All that Chuck had become and experienced was not haphazard. God had spent a lifetime combining education, passion, and experience in order to prepare Chuck for that which He had called him to. While the world may see all of these things as leading to a grand finale much like a concert, for Chuck now was the time to give as an act of worship to God. The appropriate response for Chuck was to give the Atlanta Youth Academy something they never thought they could afford or attain. He gave himself.

Questions for Reflection

Is there a leader you look up to? What do you admire most about him/her?

You may not have extra money or advanced skills, but do you know a way you could give of yourself to a local non-profit, school, or church?

5 | RECOMPENSE

With Chuck Johnston as it president, the school gained a level of notoriety and credibility they had yet to attain. For the first time since the school began, Larry believed that not only could this crazy dream of his survive but it could thrive. Chuck's presence and knowledge brought a level of organization the school desperately needed in order to maintain its growth.

As with all ventures, there are stages of development. God called Larry to start this school and he gathered a group of people around him to do everything needed to make it work. They were driven because to them this was the "right thing to do." Chuck had come to take the school to the next level. He formalized the school by codifying its mission, vision, and developing procedural standards.

Shortly after Chuck arrived the school simply outgrew their space in Glencastle. The school was in an awkward phase. They knew they could no longer stay in the old debtor's prison, but they were not in a place to develop a campus of their own. Yet, they felt that such a campus was on the horizon. They talked about it; they dreamed about it. But, they were forced to live in a time of limbo and waiting.

From Glencastle, the school moved to the campus of East Lake United Methodist Church. The church was a small urban congregation with an abundance of space. The academy worked out an agreement to rent and renovate a wing of the education building. Here in this temporary space, Chuck continued to assure a successful learning environment for each student. His diligence and commitment to excellence was not in vain. The school continued to grow.

After a few short years in the "wilderness" of a rented facility, leaders of the academy began to once again dream of a "promised land." The dream this time, however, was birthed out of necessity rather than simple desire. Chuck and others had led the school to a point where they had over-filled every classroom in the education wing of East Lake UMC. What were their options?

The academy had expanded in size, scope and impact but was still living paycheck to paycheck. The thought of raising funds to buy land and build their own campus seemed goliath in stature. When faced with such insurmountable odds, we often begin looking for logical solutions. The church had another wing vacant. It would, however, require the investing of any and all funds that could potentially be used to build their own campus one day. This additional wing had been vacant for years and was only inhabited by decades of accumulated junk and flocks of pigeons that called it home. Despite its flaws, it would afford the academy what it needed, more space.

Larry went to a storage shed at his home. There he dug out an old presentation board. The board had been used years ago to display large vacant lots located in lower income, inner city Atlanta communities. With his typical cocktail of naiveté, courage, and faith, he took this board and began dreaming of what could be.

If you're going to dream, dream big! One property stood out as an amazing possibility. It was a twenty-seven acre tract owned by FCS Urban Ministries located in the community of Norwood Manor. Norwood Manor sits in the deep southeast part of the city just on the outskirts of Atlanta's downtown business district. Few of Atlanta's northsiders would know of the community if not for "Trash Mountain", the city's largest dump or the Starlight Six, the last remaining drive-in theater in the city limits. Of all the places and all the properties, it is here that Larry felt the best place to develop a Christ centered institution of higher education.

Atlanta does not lack for private education opportunities. In fact, there are magazines and conferences devoted solely to the private education community of Atlanta. What Larry desired was not to add to the plethora of private school options. Instead he envisioned a place that would come alongside a community and strengthen the fabric of its culture. Many institutions (schools, businesses, and even churches) seek out communities that are an asset to them. What does this community have to offer to help me succeed. Rather, Larry sought out and believed God was calling the Atlanta Youth Academy to develop itself in a community where he and they could be a valid and needed asset.

With hopes and dreams filling his mind, the reality was he stood in front of a large piece of property that he neither owned nor had the money to purchase. Larry immediately contacted his old friend Bob Lupton, president of FCS Ministries, deed holder of the land. Bob explained to Larry he needed $180k for the property in order to invest in another ministry venture they were beginning. While $180k was an amazing deal for 27 acres, it was money the Academy did not have.

Over the next two months Larry shared the good news with friends of the ministry who had means. All agreed the property had potential, but no one agreed enough to write a check. Larry, like many founders, was selling a vision with no firm development plan to back it up – it was deemed "risky."

He recalls it was a Thursday morning when he received a phone call from Bob telling him that two different developers were coming over the next day, both wanting to sign a contract on the property. All things being equal, he wanted the academy to have the property, but Bob needed his answer within the next 24 hours. His answer, of course, was that he wanted the property - he just didn't have any way to pay for it. He had knocked on every door he knew to knock and was finally at the end of his resources.

Friday morning came and Larry was on the phone with Thad Warren. Thad was a childhood friend from school and church. He had served on the ministry board of the Atlanta Youth Project and they were discussing a program at Thad's church. In the middle of the conversation, with a by-the-way manner, Thad asked, "did you get that land you were looking at?"

Thad had walked the property with Larry a month earlier. "Funny you should ask," Larry replied, told him about the conversation with Bob, and explained that in two hours the opportunity would be gone.

"How much do you need?" asked Thad.

"$180,000," said Larry.

Thad responded, "Wow, I don't have that kind of money."

Hopefully Larry inquired, "Do you know anybody who does."

"My dad would, do you want me to ask him?" Larry gulped and stammered. "Larry, Dad is standing at the door with his jacket in his hand ready to go to the farm for the weekend, do you want me to ask him?

"Yes," said Larry with a shaky voice.

"Ok, I will call you back," Thad hung up.

Larry immediately stopped and prayed. Larry tells of how he prayed in the same way you do when you are driving and your gas needle is below empty. He prayed an intense, focused, singular request, "Lord, please!"

Thad's father, Ray Warren, called back with one request for Larry, to "get on his knees and pray" and to ask the board of directors to pray as well. If God was telling them that this is where the school "needs" to be, then Larry should come by his office next Tuesday morning and they will "make it happen."

Larry prayed. Larry called the board to pray. They discerned this is where the school needed to be. It was not that this particular wooded tract in the middle of an urban neighborhood was the most logical place for a school. The neighborhood was certainly not the safest place for children and families. They would encounter resistance from many people, including those who did not wish to shine a light on the more shady activities of their community. But Mr. Warren's request was not to pray for where you want to be or where everyone thinks you should be. Before Mr. Warren was going to front his finances, he wanted Larry to confidently discern this is where the Academy *needed* to be.

Larry arrived at the office where Mr. Warren had decided to put up stock as security for a loan with SunTrust Bank that would allow the academy to purchase the acreage. In Larry's mind the hard work had been accomplished. He had secured the purchase of the future home of Atlanta Youth Academy. His glow, however, was short lived.

Not long after closing, Larry added a new word to his vocabulary- recompense fee. It is a word most urban developers know and have come to fear. It is the fee the city of Atlanta imposes to compensate for every tree removed within city limits. It was an important word to know considering Larry had just purchased 27 acres of densely wooded property.

In an initial meeting with a general contractor, Larry was explained the recompense process. His heart sank with fear. The builder assured him it could not be that bad, it is just part of the cost of doing business inside the city limits of Atlanta. With a brief glance of the land plan, he informed Larry the fee might be in the $100k range. $100k neither Larry nor the academy had. To set Larry's mind at ease the contractor promised to send someone out to the property to do a random tree survey and develop a more accurate figure.

The night, however, was going to get darker before the dawn. A few days later Larry got the phone call, "are you sitting down?" The tree audit of the property determined the actual recompense fee to be $1.2 million. Larry had just convinced the academy to purchase a piece of property which, for all practical purposes, would be deemed useless because they could not even afford to clear the trees. Gloom abounded.

But like dawn breaking in at the darkest part of the night, Larry was informed he could appeal the fee. So, with the tree survey professional, Chuck Johnson, and some praying friends, he set off to go before the city's recompense fee board. They were last on the day's docket. So, they sat.

First up was a gentleman from Buckhead who sought to appeal his fee for removing two trees that were entangled and a threat to his home. He was swiftly denied. Larry and his team watched person after person appeal with a maximum success of fif-teen percent deducted from their fees. Even at that percentage, the future of the Academy's plans seemed dead in the water.

Finally, the Atlanta Youth Academy was called forward. Larry began to make a moving case for the work the academy was performing in the lives of children in the city and explain why they could not afford to pay the fee. Seeing the fortune of those who had gone before, Chuck and the friends that came with him sat fervently praying in the back of the hearing room.

The first to speak on behalf of the tree board was its lone African American member who happen to live in a neighboring community of the school. Standing, he expressed a belief in the worthy goal of the school and felt the money for the fee would be better invested in the children. As he was sitting down the member next to him said “why don’t you make it a motion?”

He then made a motion to completely dissolve the fee. Every hand raised in favor and Larry’s jaw dropped. Unanimously the board had agreed to waive the fee! AYA had received its first million-dollar gift.

It had now been over six months since Larry had initially visited Ray Warren’s office to discuss the property, the “Promised Land” as they called it. With a sense of excitement, Larry returned to share the news with Mr. Warren. They basked together in the hopeful future of the school. He agreed with Larry that now was the time to begin a capital campaign. With the recompense fee gone it now cleared the way to approach major donors and do the hard work of planning and building a campus.

Larry left the meeting joyful of the outcome and possessed a sense of security because of what Mr. Warren brought to the table. He had assured Larry he would personally contact his friends of means and they would work together to see this campus built.

Two weeks later, Larry received a phone call that Mr. Warren had been taken to the hospital. Larry rushed over to Piedmont Hospital to be with his friend and greatest supporter. He was too late. Mr. Warren was dead.

Questions for Reflection

Describe a time you faced a challenge you never thought you would overcome?

How did you see the hand of God in the resolution?

6 | VISION

God said to Abram,

"As for me, this is my covenant with you: You will be the father of many nations. No longer will you be called Abram; your name will be Abraham, for I have made you a father of many nations. I will make you very fruitful; I will make nations of you, and kings will come from you. I will establish my cove-nant as an everlasting covenant between me and

you and your descendants after you for the generations to come, to be your God and the God of your descendants after you. The whole land of Canaan, where you now reside as a foreigner, I will give as an everlasting possession to you and your descendants after you; and I will be their God." Genesis 17: 4-8

This promise to Abram would seem grand enough within any context. To make it even more amazing, Abram is ninety-nine years old, his wife is past childbearing age, and he is living as a nomad. God is casting a vision for Abram, not only one that speaks to the grandeur of God's hopes and dreams for him but also for his descendants in perpetuity.

The covenant is God's, but within the overall vision are imbedded responsibilities for Abram as well. He is to change his name to Abraham and undergo circumcision, no small deal for a man of his age. He is to conceive nations through his barren, elderly wife and is to be faithful and blameless before God. All visionary successes have an origin point and God gave Abraham the initial responsibility to cultivate a culture where he and his descendants will work hard to live into the hope God had for the people.

The story of the Atlanta Youth Project is essentially the story of two visions. First, Larry's vision for a private Christian school excelling to the highest academic levels to be built in a lower income, urban community. Larry envisions future civic, religious, and business leaders developing their foundations within the walls of this academic institution. He envisions a campus able to maintain a student body of 480 children.

The second, and perhaps more important vision, is the story of the countless visions being cast for the children of the school. Although the students come from diverse backgrounds, each hears the message that God created in them, with intentionality, a plan of hope and a future. Casting such a vision can not be taken lightly; those who raise the hopes of under-resourced children of the city have a major responsibility to God and to the children.

Just as Abram and his descendants, Larry, the teachers, parents and students of the Atlanta Youth Academy are creating a holy covenant as they dreamed of God's hopes for both their school and the children. Each would hold responsibility in that covenant and only time would tell if they were committed to cultivating a culture where both the school and the students could successfully live into that vision.

After only a few years in the rented education wing of a church, the Atlanta Youth Academy had simply out grown their current facility and needed to make major logistical changes in order to maintain growth. What makes the academy worthy of investing millions of dollars in the development of a campus? Why not remain a nomadic school? What value could a campus bring to the students, the community, and the academy as an institution?

One of the core tenets of AYA is that it is a Christian school. That does not mean it is a school for Christians. In fact, the academy is committed to not being a covenant school. This means no student is required to sign a statement of faith as a requirement for attendance. AYA is Christian in how it cast a vision for and with the students of the school.

The foundational soil from which the school grows is the belief that every child is created with intentionality in the image of God for Kingdom work in this world. As a Christian school the gospel is continually and creatively presented to the students. They are taught from a biblical viewpoint how to think through important questions like "Who am I?" and "Where am I going (in life and in eternity)?" The Atlanta Youth Academy is a Christian school in that they cast a theocentric vision for their students. It is the God given responsibility of the entire AYA family to create a culture that gives all involved the opportunity to live into that vision of success. For the leaders of the academy, this means creating a culture different than the culture at large.

Larry reports hearing children in the community, who were not attending the school, refer to it as the "proper speaking school." Such a moniker speaks to the success of the school but also the disparity within the culture at large. According to the US Education Department, there is a "frustratingly wide" gap between black and white students.[iii] The reasons for this gap are numerous. Some of these factors occur at home, such as the amount of television viewing in comparison to talking and positive interaction with adults. Some factors occur at school. Reports show schools with high minority rates receive less public funding and less tenured teachers than majority white schools. Some factors are cultural, such as the stigma of being smart, reading, or being "too white."

There is little the academy could do to immediately change the home and overall culture in which their students live. The academy could, however, be a place of respite from those societal pressures and in that respite develop an alternative culture where academics are celebrated, hard work is rewarded, and inappropriate behavior is swiftly disciplined.

This alternative culture certainly did not run counter to the hopes of a growing number of parents and grandparents who sought out the academy for their children. These loving guardians wanted nothing but the best for their kids. Thus, Larry and Chuck felt the academy had a responsibility to create a place where these students could live up to the highest bar of expectation.

Since first meeting in the basement of an old prison, then in the abandoned wing of a Methodist Church, the leadership of the Atlanta Youth Academy had been working hard to develop a culture in which students from the harshest of backgrounds could dream and pursue a vision for what God may have in store for them. This culture begins with the academy's board and is cultivated by a highly motivated and passionate faculty and staff. Larry explains that the academy searches out young talented teachers who want to change the world and then gives them that opportunity.

The level of excellence in administration brought to the table by President Chuck Johnston is a significant part of the success of AYA. The academic bar set by Chuck, however, could not have been implemented without the competent and capable leadership of a successful principal. For years, Chuck wad blessed to serve alongside Derrick Lockwood, principal and now Dean of the Atlanta Youth Academy.

Prior to the academy, Derrick served as vice-principal of a successful Charter school in Atlanta. As winner of the coveted "DeKalb Teacher of the

Year" award, he was set to work his way up the ranks of administration, but he desired more. As a person of faith, Derrick sought a place where his faith could actively come alongside a high level of academic leadership. Like many who had the opportunity to pursue success in other realms, Derrick understood success must be defined in relation to God's vision for our life, not others visions or understandings of success.

With capable leadership in place that demonstrated academic excellence, the academy needed to determine who their competition would be. From early on, the Atlanta Youth Academy set out to do more than just offer an alternative to the local public inner city school. The academy always sought to cast a vision for itself and for its students that was competitive with the best private schools in the city. Thus, the standards for students, teachers, and staff at AYA was and continuous to be the highest standards of academic excellence, rivaling any private education institution.

Every student at the academy is required to wear a uniform. Children are taught in a 12:1 ratio assuring that every child is given quality instructional and assessment attention. Children and their parents are responsible for discipline with behavior and truancy both being grounds for expulsion from the academy.

After touring the new campus of a private Christian school on the affluent north side of Atlanta, Larry was burdened more than ever that an academic campus was going to be essential to creating a culture worthy of the vision they were casting. For Larry a campus would not only allow the school to serve a greater number of students with sports fields and amenities, but also foster the culture of success it was striving to attain.

Additionally a campus could offer a place of stability for those students from transitional home situations. The academy could be the one place of structure and consistency in their lives. Larry hoped for a physical location with all the beauty of a private school, not for vanity sake, but to be a reflection of the value of the students who attend. A campus that is symbolic of the importance of education and an environment that affirms and nurtures the intrinsic worth of every child.

As the academy began to grow and hone their vision to be one of the best private schools in the city, they needed a method to discern for themselves and express to their students whether or not they were achieving their academic goals. The academy began to measure its academic achievements not on the same scales as the public school, but on the far more strenuous ERB scale (used by many private schools).

Larry, Chuck, and Derrick had assembled a talented leadership team, and the students were faithful in their studies and dressed for success in their uniforms every day. Other than the lack of a campus of their own, the academy looked and acted like a private school of the highest measure. But, were they performing academically? An outside educational consultant came in to examine the school. After an independent assessment, the consultant concluded that after a student has been in the school for three years they are achieving success in the top 50% percentile of of schools on the ERB scale.

The consultant's findings not only validated the hard work of the leaders and commitment of the students, but it also reflected the generosity of those who funded the academy. Success was now tangible, but new challenges lingered on the horizon. Would success at the academy equal success outside of the school culture? Could an AYA student achieve the same level of success in the resourced private school environment that the academy had strove to replicate? What happens to the students academically and socially once they leave the safe confines of the school after the eighth grade? As the first classes began to graduate into high school, time would tell.

Questions for Reflection

What do you believe is the vision of God for your life?

What do you need to do and/or change to create a culture that allows you to live fully into that vision?

7 | HOLY WORK

Ps 68:5 - A father to the fatherless, a defender of widows, is God in his holy dwelling. (NIV)

And time began to tell....

Carolyn Ouya was a student at the Atlanta Youth Academy. Her mother was a maid and her father died while she was still in junior high. She was the picture of an inner city child who should have fallen through the cracks. But Principal Lockwood made every effort to assure she grew up and was shaped by the academy's culture of success. After eighth grade she won a scholarship to Miss Porter High School in Connecticut, one of the best all girls' private schools in the country. Statistically this young woman had a much greater chance of growing up into a life of teenage pregnancy and poverty than graduating with honors from the same high school where young women from the Vanderbilt, Kennedy, and Bush families had attended.

Keenon Rush graduated from the Atlanta Youth Academy and was accepted into the prestigious McCallie High School in Chattanooga, Tennessee. He had only played flag football at AYA before becoming the first African American starting quarterback in McCallie's one hundred year history. Upon graduating from McCallie he earned the opportunity to be a student athlete at Wake Forest University. Keenon recalls his experience at AYA: "When I started high school at McCallie, I wasn't sure what to expect. Soon I realized, that God had used my teachers and AYA to intentionally equip me with all the academic and spiritual tools I needed. I've not only made the Headmaster's list for earning all A's, but I'm also the starting quarterback for our 5A football team. The Lord has blessed me in so many ways."

Albert Wilson was the first graduate of AYA to attend a private boarding school, receiving a $28k a year scholarship. Jakobi Scroggins after graduating AYA and high school is now excelling academically as a chemistry and psychology major at Mar's Hill College. Jordan Arnold left AYA to attend Blair Academy in New Jersey and is currently interviewing with fine arts schools such as Juilliard. Anthony Gates left AYA to attend Whitefield Academy on the north side of Atlanta and is now focused on academics and excelling at Morehouse College.

The academy is proud of its numerous and ongoing success stories, but it is also true that not every student is able to easily transition out of the academy into a differing racial and socio economic school. There have been accounts of AYA alumni who have been teased, mocked, and even one had another student defecate in their book bag.

Larry tells the story of one intelligent and gifted young alumnus who grew up in a family where his father was in and out of prison. Upon graduating he was blessed to receive a scholarship affording him the opportunity to attend a $15k+ annual tuition high school. As one could imagine, the culture background of the majority of students from this prep school were intrinsically different from those of AYA. Overall he was doing well at the school. But early on he was picked on by a few of his class mates as teenagers will often do to someone who is "different." Unable to bear it, this young man expressed himself in a way possibly more tolerable in his home culture but not understood or tolerated at all in his new. He was expelled.

Though his expulsion was later reversed, emotionally he could not go back. Regardless of the long-term academic benefits and social connections this school could afford him, the damage had been done. Instead, he attended a public school in his neighborhood, where he excelled like so many other students from AYA and is now attending college.

For AYA, a far more glamorous achievement is that to date, 100% of the students coming out of 8th grade have graduated from high school with 94% percent of them going off to college. Nearly no public inner city junior high school can boast of such academic success.

With all its worldly accomplishments one might ask, is the work of the Atlanta Youth Academy holy? As the pastor of a local congregation, I find a sense of holiness in what I do each week as I proclaim a message, serve the elements of communion, and baptize new believers. I get a sense of participating with God in this world. But does the door of the church mark the line between the sacred and secular?

Jesus proclaimed his purpose as healing the sick, delivering a message of good news to the poor and proclaiming freedom for the prisoner. Jesus was seeking to work with people caught in the bondage and oppression that can occur within all cultural realities. Teachers at the academy are casting a vision for their students of a life that does not include poverty and prison. Many of the students, however, live within generational cycles of scarcity: scarcity of money, education, job potential, and most devastatingly hope. Is there a God given responsibility to follow such vision casting with the hard work of making the fulfillment of that vision a reality? Is that work holy?

Urban ministry pioneer Bob Lupton writes about a mission phenomenon he describes as *toxic charity*[iv]. In his assessment, the church all too often simply "gives" to the poor in the name of Christ. He holds this over-generosity up against "equipping" people to vision, work, and achievement on their own. After decades of living in the inner city, Lupton has come to believe the latter is the more difficult but the truer work of God. He believes indulgent giving may make the giver feel good but can hurt the recipients by developing a culture of dependence rather than growth. Thus *charity*, even in the name of Christ, can be *toxic* in its long-term affects.

While his evaluation may seem controversial, decades of wealthy, suburban churches soaking the inner city with money, stuff, and a hollow vision of a better future have proven largely unfruitful. Far too regularly Larry was still seeing kids dropping out of school, violence tearing families apart, and unwise decisions landing smart young adults with great potential in prison.

Building prisons in order to house an ever-growing incarcerated population is big business in the United States. In some ways the building of prisons is a self-fulfilling prophecy. Federal and state governments build larger and larger prisons anticipating that there will be inmates to fill the beds. Judges convict persons to prison as long as beds exist. It is not until the prison population is overflowing that serious alternative measures are engaged as a stopgap until more prison cells are constructed. And then the cycle repeats.

How does the government predict how many prison cells to construct? Determining a future prison population is a well studied and calculated science. California, Texas and others specifically plan the amount of prison bed based on the number of fourth graders not reading at level.[v] Study after study has linked poverty, race, and illiteracy to future incarceration.[vi]

The heart of AYA's mission is to be amongst communities that statistically would provide the city of Atlanta with an above average percentage of its future inmates. It is strategically positioned to do something the local public schools desires but is all too often unsuccessful and the church hopes for but is not positioned to do — break the cycle of poverty and illiteracy. The academy understands what prison builders already know; failure to read at grade level greatly enhances the likelihood of imprisonment in the future of a child's life.

The Atlanta Youth Academy sought to solve the problem in a very different way, perhaps a more holy way. Rather than building more prisons to hold more people, AYA sought to provide freedom from bondage by assuring every single child at their school could read at grade level and provided them with access to educational success rarely afforded to someone of their income bracket.

It is too early to determine what long-term impact the Atlanta Youth Academy is having and will have on the culture at large. But if one uses child literacy rates as a determinate measure for the number of prison cells to construct, then the Atlanta Youth Academy has done their part in lowering that number.

Principal Derrick Lockwood describes how the academy is changing cultural paradigms and moving generational blinders that would hinder the students from seeing and experience all God might have in store for them. When Derrick arrived at AYA in 2003, 16 of his students where on the verge of failing and 40 of them had missed over 30 days of school. He knew he would be abandoning these children academically and hindering their potential to glorify God if he did not take drastic action.

Derrick had worked in inner city schools before; he knew that the kids who fall through the cracks are the ones picked up by the gangs, become involved with drugs or prostitution, and eventually land in jail. He quickly instituted a high expectation, no excuse truancy policy. Derrick has taught the children the importance of both service and success. He has exposed them to volunteer opportunities in their own community and taken them to high-rise CEO offices throughout the city. He continues to work hard so that every student can clearly articulate their individualized answer to the question, "what is my purpose?"

According to Jesus' vision in Luke 4:18, AYA is holy work: to preach good news to the poor, to proclaim freedom for the prisoners and recovery of sight for the blind, to release the oppressed! Christians are certainly not the only ones doing good work in the world. But, when people of faith involve themselves in the things Jesus describes as holy, there is a heightened awareness of their participation in God's Kingdom work. Such awareness has the potential to turn what some see as a secular task into a sacred and holy one.

Questions for Reflection

How could God use you at your job to further God's Kingdom here on earth?

How could you help one child improve his/her odds of never landing in a jail cell?

8 | GOD'S TIMING

With so many signs of success, Larry was excited about the outlook of the academy. A sustainable future for the institution seemed to be in reach through the acquisition of the property. In addition, graduates were on track, proving academic viability. The financial hurdles of taking the next steps, though, were quickly approaching.

With the passing of Mr. Warren, Larry's greatest encouragement for a capital campaign, movements toward the dream of a new campus started off much slower than hoped. Larry was forced to swallow his pride and approached Mr. Warren's widow in order to ask for an extension of the loan that her husband had arranged for the school. She graciously agreed.

In this same time frame, ten acres of land adjoining the twenty-seven the school had already purchased came up for sale in a sealed bid auction. Feeling confident God was on his side, Larry developed a plan to acquire the land. He contacted his friend in real estate and prepared a bid. His friend educated Larry on a strategy to help them feel out the other bids and increase their chances of winning. Larry appreciated his advice but informed him that he was submitting his bid in faith.

The possibility of additional land opened up a whole new outlet for Larry to dream. It inspired Larry to develop a separate non-profit development organization called Community Village. His goal in attaining this extra land would be to develop what he calls an "academic village."

For Larry, this village would stand alongside the academy's campus and help under gird the culture of academic excellence they were already attaining. The goals of, eventually named, Community Village were to develop affordable housing within a very nice gated apartment community. A community in which families of the academy students could live. It would make it possible for students to easily walk to and from school. In addition, there could be a youth ministry staff living in the complex providing spiritual and pastoral support to the children and their families.

The final day came, the winner was announced and Community Village did not win the bid. Larry was frustrated and disappointed. The property would have allowed him to develop what he believed to be a unique and amazing opportunity for the families of the academy.

It is always unnerving when our plans of faith do not blossom in the way we hoped and doors seem to close for reasons we do not understand. And, despite the cliché, windows do not always seem to immediately open. Perhaps it is never about providing doors and windows through which we are to travel. Maybe at times God is simply initiating a missional imagination that we are to employ where we stand.

Despite the extra ten acres falling through, Larry had a passion for the development of the housing project alongside the school. He continued to keep the wheels of this idea ever turning. But the more pressing issues remained, the academy still needed to figure out a way to pay off the land they had already acquired.

After initial designs were developed for the site, the board determined they only needed half of the property to achieve their goals. This realization freed up fourteen acres of which could be sold to potentially pay off the balance owed. The academies small but generous donor base was already burdened, so selling off part of the property seemed to be the only viable option to raise the near $200k needed soon.

Despite the growing success of the school, operating funds were very tight. There were months when the payroll was barely being dispersed to the faculty and staff. For this reason, Larry could not in good conscience raise money for land when salary responsibilities were barely being met. Approaching school donors would put them at the risk of transferring their giving from the operation of the academy to its capital needs. Larry was living in a tension nearly all non-profit (and many for profit) leaders feel as they seek to pursue worthy goals of tomorrow while maintaining the operation of today.

One of the Atlanta Youth Project's board members arranged for Larry to take a member of a family foundation on a tour of the school and property. This is something Larry had done countless times. As usual, he showed his guest, Richard Harris, around the school, took him to the property, and articulated the financial need the academy had in order to retire the land's debt. Richard informed Larry that the family foundation he represented might be able to help in some way and promised to send him an application to apply for funding.

Months went by without any word from Richard and the meeting was a distant memory in the recesses of Larry's busy mind. One morning Larry woke up and for a reason he cannot fully explain, other than the guiding of the Spirit, all he could think about was how he had never obtained a grant application from Richard. In his office that morning, Larry called Richard. Larry was pleased to hear he had not missed the foundation's deadline, but he had to get an application to Florida by the end of the week.

Larry and Chuck diligently worked to assure the application was in on time. Then, they waited. Most foundation grants Larry and Chuck had been applying for were in the ten to fifteen thousand dollars range. Larry was aware of the reality that very few foundations give this kind of money to first time applicants, particularly ones of which they have no personal connection. The next Friday Larry was at Home Depot gathering supplies for a project when his cell phone rang. He answered to find Richard on the other line informing him the academy had received an award. Larry ask how much did the board grant, Richard responded, "All of it, $200,000."

This not only freed the school from debt, it allowed Larry's missional creativity to once again engage. Although he was discouraged when the additional ten acres he sought to purchase did not pan out, the Jeffersonian thought of having a school surrounded by student housing was still in the back of his mind. The vision of developing a community for the children with a safe, affordable, beautifully appointed housing complex sitting alongside the academy's campus once again took center stage in Larry's thoughts.

Months earlier when they were desperate for options to pay off the campus loan, the building committee had commissioned Larry to start looking for a buyer for the unused acres. The committee had proceeded with the initial steps to actualize a campus and one of its first agendas included finalizing a design for the site plan. All said and done, the designers confirmed the academy could meet its goals on only thirteen of the twenty-seven acres. That was good news, less acreage meant less grading, landscaping, etc, which in the end meant less money. In Larry's visionary mind, however, it meant more.

With that dream swirling about and fourteen acres left to work with, Larry began to cast a vision for how the development of a community village could be a win-win solution. First and foremost, the children and their families would benefit from such a development. Second, not donations, but market driven funds could be used to buy the land from the school. Again, Larry was faced with another monumental vision he was not prepared or equipped to handle. Multi-family, multi-million dollar apartment developments are for the big dogs, not for a youth minister who has a vision and a passion to serve the downtrodden.

For in this hope we were saved. But hope that is seen is no hope at all. Who hopes for what they already have? But if we hope for what we do not yet have, we wait for it patiently. In the same way, the Spirit helps us in our weakness. We do not know what we ought to pray for, but the Spirit himself intercedes for us through wordless groans. And he who searches our hearts knows the mind of the Spirit, because the Spirit intercedes for God's people in accordance with the will of God. And we know that in all things God works for the good of those who love him, who have been called according to his purpose. Romans 8:24-28

Paul is writing to fellow followers of Christ that are long suffering and in need of a message of hope. He is assuring them that when they have been called and are seeking God faithfully, they are not afflicted with haphazard chance, but can step with expectant hope into the future. Paul describes the Spirit as one that searches, knows, and then petitions the Father on our behalf even for that which we have yet to fully comprehend.

As Larry began to research what he thought was a great and original idea, he encountered other people of faith who had similar dreams of well built, ministry oriented, affordable apartment complexes. One of those missionally creative thinkers was Noel Khalil, President of Columbia Residential. Larry had a vision and partnered with Noel's expertise to make it happen. In a way that only God can, the Lord also brought to the table a general contractor, Barry Teague of Walton Communities. All three shared the same vision of what this village could and should be.

The academy proceeded to sell a portion of the property to the community development arm charged with building the apartment complex. The sale not only set in motion the dream of an academic village, but allowed the school to clear all debt, and be in a position to officially launch the academy into capital campaign mode with money actually in the bank! For Larry and AYA it was one of those circumstances that no one could have set out to plan, but which worked together for the good of all.

In 2006, Constitution Apartments opened its doors with 168 units available for rent on a gated, well manicured property sitting in the midst of one of Atlanta's most poverty stricken neighborhoods. Today, there is a waiting list which includes students from the school whose families seek to live in this unique enclave of living, learning, and hope.

The land began as an empty piece of land that Larry had no idea how the academy could afford, but now, it was being transformed and developed into a whole community where families will be provided with transformational stability. Children will grow and be educated in safety, and lives will be changed. On top of the intrinsic goodness of that project alone, building the complex afforded the academy the ability to start a capital campaign. Larry could not have known from the onset how to pray for what would become of this property. In faith on bended knees through the request of his now departed friend's father, Larry had inquired of the Lord if this is where they "needed to be." In hindsight he now reflects back and sees just how involved the Lord was in this process of working out good for those that are called according to God's purposes.

Larry proclaims he did not see God act in one monumental revelation or command, but time and time again the Lord demonstrated a validation of the vision. The development of the academy, or their journey to the "Promise Land," is not something that could have occurred by mere chance or random good fortune, but only by the hand of a loving God actively involved with God's people to bring the Kingdom to bear in this world. Though only God may fully know the details, as people of faith, we are called to step boldly towards the horizon of future possibility.

9 | GOD'S TIMING CONTINUED

Nearly the same time as Larry was seeing God act in God's own way for the apartment complex. Chuck Johnston was having his own crisis of faith as he raised the operational funds for the school. Chuck needed to see God work in God's own and perfect way.

Chuck was not only an accomplished leader; he was a person of great spiritual maturity. Spiritual leaders, however, are not super heroes. Since childhood, Chuck has kept a daily journal. As I researched in preparation to tell this story, I was privy to some of Chuck's most honest and personal reflections though the reading of his journal. With his permission, below are parts of his entries during a particularly difficult time of leadership for the Academy. He began the week not knowing how he was going to fund payroll or rent. He would go on to say he had no "rabbit's to pull out of his hat." He was at one of those crossroads where he had nothing to lean on but his faith in a God he knew was calling him to this work.

I include these excerpts because I found the honest struggle of a Godly, spiritually mature man to be encouraging in the pain and honest doubt we all experience. As a pastor and someone who has been forced to raise funds and at times question how the ministry bills are going to be paid, my heart softened and eyes swelled as I read Chuck's intimate cries unto God. You may never be responsible for raising funds for a large ministry, but you have probably been at that place where you are unsure of the next step. You have probably been at the place where the promise of Romans 8:24-28 is the only source of strength you can muster. There you are never alone.

Below are the personal writings of Chuck Johnston from May 2004.

Sunday, May 9, 2004

They did not thirst when He led them through the deserts; He made water flow for them from the rock; He split the rock and water gushed out. Isaiah 48:21

May God pour financial blessings down on AYA in the month of May!

Monday, May 10, 2004

"It [the kingdom of God] is like a mustard seed, which is the smallest seed you plant in the ground. Yet when planted, it grows and becomes the largest of all garden plants."

Jesus in Mark 4:31-2

I am now only seeing a shadow of what constitutes the kingdom of God. I must break out of the "routine" of my daily life and better grasp the "wonder" of it all.

... After about 2 am I slept lightly. My psyche may think I still have lots of money to raise.

Tuesday, May 11, 2004

. ... I had a touch of a headache going into my night's sleep. I ended up not sleeping well past 2 am. I think I'm somewhat worried about my lack of leadership for the board.

May God enable us to reach those who have given in the past, to see them give again.

Wednesday, May 12, 2004

And if all this had been too little, I would have given you even more. ... Then David said to Nathan, "I have sinned against the Lord." II Samuel 12:8, 13

David heart had grown cold towards the Lord. That happens to me. Instead of his enormous sin crushing him, it brought David back from the dead in his relationship with God. During the night when my eyes popped open with worry over this payroll (we have roughly $11k towards a need of $28k), I found myself saying, "I throw myself completely on the Lord." Then I slept again. My sin is "a heart of stone." I humbly ask God this day for a heart of flesh.

Thursday, May 13, 2004

I trust; help Thou my untrust.

Here is what I sent the trustees yesterday morning: We have roughly $11,000 in our account, and we need to have $32,000 for this Friday ($28K for payroll; $4K for rent); so we need an additional $21,000. We know of a scholarship gift ($10K) coming through the National Christian Foundation from Anne & Tim Irwin, but we may not have that by this Friday. I don't have any "rabbits in my hat" for this one.

Friday, May 14, 2004

There is more Power and guidance available through the Holy Spirit than I have yet comprehended. I must turn to Him as my counselor.

I am consumed with anticipation over how God will provide "at the last minute" the funds we need today. I cry out!

Saturday, May 15, 2004

Towards the $21K we needed for yesterday's payroll, $1K came in from Larry Teem. The miracle is that SunTrust honored PayCheck's draft.

Lord, Jesus Christ, Son of God, have mercy on me.

Sunday, May 16, 2004

Into Your hands I commit my spirit; redeem me, O Lord, the God of truth. ... But I trust in You, O Lord; I say, "You are my God." My times are in Your hands. ... Be strong and take heart, all you who hope in the Lord. Psalm 31:5, 14-15, 24

Let me truly throw myself upon the Lord. Those are nearly the words that gave me relief Wednesday morning when I woke up with fear for the financial future of AYA: *into Your hands, my times are in Your hands, take heart.*

May Atlanta Youth Academy become sanctified and supplied abundantly!!

Monday, May 17, 2004

I pray that we will not lose donors to these kids.

Tuesday, May 18, 2004

It was Monday, and last Friday (when we needed a total of $21,000) passed without sufficient funds in the bank to cover payroll and rent. There was the $1,000 gift from Larry Teem. [SunTrust honored the draft of our account by PayChecks.] There were no phone messages or e-mails waiting for me about money. We did learn later that Frank & Margaret Ann were sending $1,250, and Richard Parker was sending $1,000. I also called Mary Carroll at National Christian Foundation and found that the promised Tim & Anne Irwin gift had been requested. I went to our mailbox in East Atlanta and collected a $500 gift. Just as I was leaving to go get the $10,000 Irwin gift from National Christian Foundation, Terrell came in from our box at FCS with a $1,000 gift from Apostles and a $9,000 from Marshall & Clare Evans. The expression is that "God is seldom early but always on time." Well, it would seem as if He were a business day late with payroll & rent. My perception must be wrong. Clearly this all came together at His hand, in the right time. Praise God!

Praise God from Whom all blessings flow!

Questions for Reflection

Describe a time where you had no choice but to cry out to God?

Describe a time something has worked out for good, but not in the way you initially hoped or expected?

How can Romans 8:24-28 change how we pray for situations in our life?

10 | HOME

Selling half the original twenty-seven acres made the dream of Community Village a reality. It also allowed the trustees of the school to enter into serious conversations about building an actual campus. Any non–profit leader will tell you, it is one thing to approach a funder with a dream, but it is a completely different thing to approach a funder with a dream, no debt and substantial seed money.

With the apartment complex a go and the capital campaign poised to launch, Larry needed assurance that he had support from the student body. The new campus would be almost five miles from the academy's current rented facility. One practical fear for the board was that any move might cause undue hardships for the families potentially causing them to drop out. After several conversations and opportunities to cast a vision, Larry was thrilled when he received overwhelming support for the move from both the students and the faculty alike.

Among the entire AYA family there was an excitement about the future. Larry describes it as the same kind of excitement a family feels when they have been living in a rented apartment and then move into a home of their own. The joy of watching their new property take form was infectious and as news spread of the upcoming campus, applications to attend the academy began to increase.

The school family had certainly bought into the dream but the looming question remained: would donors come to the table? Larry and Chuck knew this project hinged upon developing a competent and energized capital campaign board. Chaired by investment banker Lee Burrows, an amazing team of men and women began to step up and support the effort.

The initial estimate for the campaign was $6.5 million. With start-up money in the bank, they took a very wise step in hiring the highly regarded Coxe Curry and Associates as consultants. John O'Kane, Coxe Curry's senior advisor, was engaged to assist them with a feasibility study to discern what they should be able to raise.

Larry is a dreamer, and the board had a passion for that dream; however, employing an organization known for helping non-profits achieve their goals brought a level of tenured wisdom regarding what the academy could realistically raise. After an in-depth assessment, the Coxe Curry team predicted the board would be able to raise $4.6 million. Although, not the amount they had initially hoped for, they heeded their consultant's advice, rolled up their sleeves and set out to accomplish the goal.

After nearly a year of families, individuals, board members, and foundations coming together - the campaign was victorious. The reality of this fundraising achievement speaks to a deeper level of success that Larry, Chuck, Derrick, and Lee had been able to achieve.

Years ago when Larry and Joel Moore were working with the struggling Christian school just a few miles up the road from where the new campus would sit; Larry was told over and over again that he needed to start a school because people give to persons, not simply projects. He also learned that people give to the level of credibility they see in the current and future vision of the ministry. In the first couple of years when the academy had less than forty students, before Chuck was recruited to join the team; Larry met with the executive director of one of Atlanta's most important foundations. This well seasoned non-profit executive loved the dream, was empathetic towards the academy's needs, but as he was leaving he phrased a simple question "how are you going to sustain it?"

"God has brought us this far, God will carry us forward." Larry replied.

He got a nice pat on the arm and a warm smile. A prophetic proclamation is not exactly what the director of a prominent foundation wants to go back and lay on the table for his board to consider.

This same executive made it a point to be involved in a substantial way in gifting to AYA's capital campaign years latter. Thus, the accomplishment of such an ambitious campaign spoke volumes to the level of trust that Larry, Chuck, and others had earned through their dedication and sacrifice to get the school off the ground. It may only take months to raise millions of dollars, but it takes years to earn the trust of donors needed to accomplish such a goal.

The school that had begun with nine students in the basement of an old debtor's prison was now moving onto the "Promised Land." Maintaining its commitment to small class size, the school immediately began operating on a waiting list and devised a plan to expand each grade level four times over to eventually achieve a capacity of 480 students.

In addition to classrooms, library, computer lab and a multi-purpose gym-a-cafe-a-auditorium, the campus opened with a full size sports field and a tennis court. Seeking to discern what was best for the children, the school sought to invest in the "lifetime sports" of soccer, tennis, and basketball. These sports could be achieved at a level of success within a small class size without losing focus on the higher goal of the school: the academic achievement of the students. These sports were also activities the children could learn and participate in throughout their lifetime, thus promoting long-term health, physicality, and community involvement. Further, these sports would hopefully help better integrate the students into the private and collegial cultures they were preparing for post-academy.

Throughout these chapters I have expressed that Atlanta Youth Academy is not a school for Christians but a Christian school. The academy is not Christian in a way, as Larry illustrates, " the answer to every question is 'Jesus.'" What makes the academy Christian is how they cast a theocentric vision for and with the students that is fundamentally rooted in the belief that each child is intentionally created by God and that God has a plan and a purpose for them upon this earth.

The Atlanta Youth Academy does not prepare students to succeed in middle-class, American life. What makes this academy Christian is its definition of success. American or world standards do not define success, but instead, students are being encouraged to know God and understand God's plan and hope for their life. These students are then given direction as they walk towards fulfilling whatever call God may place upon them. To actively participate with God in God's kingdom work here on the earth - this is success.

God may be calling some of the students to be well-known business and civic leaders. God may be calling some students to pastor congregations around the globe. God may be calling a student of the academy to lead the free world as President of the United States or to successfully battle the AIDS crisis as a missionary in Africa. God could be calling some students to marry, have children and raise them intentionally, strategically in their community as disciples of Jesus. With Christ as the center, success in life cannot be measured by anything other than the bar God sets for our lives. AYA is teaching students to hear and follow the Spirit, and providing them with a path to imitate the humble yet profound history-altering success of Christ. The academy teaches students as Paul taught the church at Philippi—to live lives worthy of the gospel of Christ.

6 Who, being in very nature God,

did not consider equality with God something to be used to his own advantage;

7 rather, he made himself nothing

by taking the very nature of a servant,

being made in human likeness.

8 And being found in appearance as a man,

he humbled himself

by becoming obedient to death—

even death on a cross!

9 Therefore God exalted him to the highest place

and gave him the name that is above every name,

10 that at the name of Jesus every knee should bow,

in heaven and on earth and under the earth,

11 and every tongue acknowledge that Jesus Christ is Lord,

to the glory of God the Father. Philippians 2:6-11

Success for Jesus was coming to be "exalted to the highest place" and given the name at which "every knee should bow." Such success did not come to him free of temptation. He had those who desired for him to simply live into the expectations of one being from Nazareth – what good could come from him. Satan tempted him to succeed by means alternative to the cross. In the garden Jesus prays in desperation for the cup to be taken from him. Many of the children of AYA live within a similar tension. Some must overcome low expectations of culture, some must overcome the lure of drugs or the easy money mindset of celebrity, and others must overcome the desire to simply give up.

The Atlanta Youth Academy does not claim to be the only institution offering education, sports programs, or mentoring for these children. The academy stands boldly with a prophetic voice to announce and teach what they believe to be a better way forward—a way forward that excludes violence, drugs, or crime. From day one they communicate that each student is created and loved by God for a purpose, and that by becoming an educated disciple of Christ you can achieve whatever God has in store for you. What makes the Atlanta Youth Academy and ultimately what should make all people who follow Jesus *Christian* is the core belief and proclamation that living a "life worthy of the gospel" is the only life worth living. Such a theology is clearly evident in the academies mission and values.

Mission

The Atlanta Youth Academy exists to advance the kingdom of God by offering an excellent Christ-centered education to underserved urban communities.

Vision

The Atlanta Youth Academy's vision is to equip the students of Atlanta's inner city with the academic tools, social skills, and high character traits necessary to afford them the opportunity of a post-high school education and a purposeful, productive and Spirit filled life. Additionally, the vision is to create a learning environment that so emulates the precepts and principles of Jesus Christ that it serves as salt and light to all who come in contact with its staff, students, and leadership.

AYA Values

* We provide students with a superior education by upholding the highest academic standards.

* We prepare students for the best academic and social futures in high school, college and beyond.

* We urge students to live up to their Christ-given potential by nurturing Christian character traits.

* We encourage, in each student, a strong sense of purpose and conviction for serving others.

* We maintain intimate class sizes in order to provide the level of personal attention each student needs.

* We look to the Lord, Jesus Christ, as the Servant Teacher and mentor students to pattern themselves after Him in all areas of life.

* Ultimately, we prepare well-rounded students poised to become the next generation of great leaders.

Questions for Reflection

What do you think living a life "worthy of the gospel" means?

Make a mission and value statement(s) for your life?

11 | NEIGHBORS

Outside of the academic realm, AYA has played an important role in the Norwood Manor community. They have been neighbors. This may seem obvious, but in fact, all Christian institutions are neighbors. Whether an institution is a church, a school, or a non-profit helping agency; the question that should always be asked is - are these "Christian" institutions good neighbors?

Communities have hopes and goals deep within their ethos. Urban communities often have a deep sense of pride and vision for what they expect in their neighborhood. Christian institutions are uniquely situated to play a significant role in the fulfillment of that vision when they work alongside neighbors to communicate and employ discerned goals. There is great power and beauty when neighbor comes alongside neighbor to achieve goals together.

Christian institutions must also realize there is great danger when they act as poor neighbors, thinking only of their own goals at the expense of the community in which they reside. Bob Lupton tells the story of a small church within a historic urban Atlanta community.[vii] A church that once acted as the house of worship for local residence brought in a dynamic and charismatic preacher. This man of God grew the church and it became a central worship center for residents from many corners of the city. Rather than walking to church, these new worshippers drove, worshipped, and left. On the surface this seems to bear no harm on the community.

A common urban issue quickly arose, parking. Out of necessity, the church began to purchase nearby homes with the plan to raze them and add much needed parking. The community, upset at the potential of empty asphalt lots littering their community six out of seven days a week caused a backlash. The community and the church quickly became fierce opponents of one another, each believing the other was selfishly seeking its own agenda without regard for the other.

Seasoned with the dynamics of urban communities, Larry knew for the AYA to be a success he had to gain not only the allowance of the Norwood Manor community, but their support. He did not desire for neighbors to simply see the project as an altruistic venture, but a positive step for the development of the community. Thus, before construction of the academy began, Larry began at local pastor, Monte Norwood's, office.

Monte is the senior pastor of the Bible Way Ministries International Church. He is the third generation of Norwood's to have a prominent role in the community that bears his family name. In the early 1900's, his grandfather, Robert Norwood, developed what came to be known as Norwood Manor.

Robert was a successful African American businessman, builder, and real estate developer. After the turn of the century he began to buy up land in what was at that time, the distant southeast corner of Atlanta. He slowly began to sell lots and build modest homes for African American families. Quickly, Norwood Manor became a distinct community of vibrant black culture.

Robert's wife and a few other women began a door to door bible study and prayer meeting. They would literally stop by house after house teaching scripture and inquiring how they might pray for the household. This creative ministry developed into a church. Robert's son and Monte's father, Matthew, eventually became pastor of the church. He held this prominent role in the community for many years until his son, Monte, succeed him as senior pastor.

Anyone working in the city will tell you, you must understand the formal and informal power structures of a community. For Norwood Manor, both of those include members of the Norwood family. Formally, power in the community is displayed through the Norwood Civic Association. To be successful there, Larry knew he must do his due diligence in the local pastoral offices.

Monte describes the hesitancies that the neighborhood leaders had to Larry and AYA coming into the community. Like many urban communities, Larry was not the first seemingly rich white Christian ready to save the neighborhood.

From his experience nothing seems to please resourced Christians more than developing and implementing a program to save the "other"- whether that "other" be in a far away village or an urban community. It is conveniently pleasing to suburbanites if that program can be implemented by a volunteer team on a Saturday or as part of a week long mission trip. Monte does not want to negate the value of work from well-intentioned volunteers, but only to suggest that often commitment is of equal importance to message.

Too often Christians helicopter into a community without discerned regard for local wisdom, assistance, and/or support. At times, such acts in the name of Christ can cause harm. The global and technological culture in which we live allows Christians to act and react to issues with unprecedented speed and enthusiasm.

In his book, *The Hole In our Gospel*, Richard Sterns warns of such ill-discerned reactionary measures by Christians.[viii] In Africa, malaria, often contracted from bug bites during sleep, is a severe health epidemic. Thus, numerous agencies are seeking to help every family attain a net to place around their bed. One group of Americans felt compassion for the issue and decided to solve the problem by purchasing and bringing hundreds of sleeping nets to a certain village. This group failed to realize a community of indigenous Africans had started a net making business which employed local workers and used local supplies. The native people were working to solve the issue, as well as bolster the communities' economy. As it turned out, the church group came in handing out hundreds of nets, while at the same time wrecking a local economic cycle thus sending a large group of Africans back into poverty...all in the name of Jesus.

Within global and urban communities, the savior mentality of outsiders has caused indigenous people to develop an understandable sense of guard when approached with plans to "help" the community. Larry certainly encountered such hesitancies. In fact, Larry was not the first to propose the building of a private school in the area. The civic association had already expended effort to support a school, which only proved unsuccessful.

Larry worked to gain the trust and support of both Monte and his father, Bishop Matthew Norwood. Seeing the level of success that the academy had already attained, the Bishop championed the cause as an upgrade for the community, particularly given the current dynamics of Norwood Manor.

Prior to the development of the apartments and the academy, Norwood Manor had experienced decades of decline as many of the young residents had moved out and away from their families. As the older adults left or passed away, houses become vacant, luring in those with less than noble intentions. Many saw and hoped for AYA to bring kids back to the community, giving direction and purpose to the community, and deterring the ever present loitering.

It is evident the Atlanta Youth Academy has excelled in academic goals. The academy had successfully raised capital and built a great campus. But, had they (and are they) a good neighbor? I cannot help but wonder how often churches and other Christian institutions fail to ask this question of themselves.

One reason I have chosen to write this story is because I believe AYA can stand with pride and say they have been good neighbors. They have intentionally developed their property with the community in mind. The AYA campus is regularly open for community flag football and youth basketball leagues as well as an annual health fair. The apartment community they built is a beautiful addition that provides safe and affordable housing for residents of Norwood Manor. These residents in turn are active, transformational parts of the community. So much so, the current president of the Norwood Civic Association resides in the apartment village.

Due to its board, faculty, and alumni, the reality is that AYA, as an institution, can carry a powerful voice within city politics. In some ways, a more powerful voice than the residents of the neighborhood could carry individually or even collectively.

The academy has been a good steward of that voice to defend against those that may seek to take advantage of the small voice one community may have in sea of political sway.

This stewardship is most evident in the academy standing alongside the neighborhood to fight a waste transfer station. Norwood Manor is a residential community, but in terms of land use it is plagued with large tracts of commercially zoned property. For years, individuals of influence have sought to place a large trash transfer station on one of the tracts that sits amongst residences. It seemed to be a matter of time before the transfer station would eventually win. With the development of the Atlanta Youth Academy, the fight against a station gained a powerful ally.

Christian institutions should never blindly support community initiatives. Yet, as organized people of faith we do have a responsibility to use our position as high-profile neighbors to speak against actions that will be detrimental to our communities. Our voice may speak to such tangible realties as unfairness based upon race or economic status, poorly planned gentrification, or a trash transfer station in the middle of a residential neighborhood.

Students and their families have intentionally moved into the Norwood Manor community, increasing the presence of young families. Pastor

Norwood reports he has seen a drop in loitering on the streets. In the name of Christ, the Atlanta Youth Academy has become an agent of positive transformation in the community. In essence, they have become close to how Jesus describes a neighbor.

But a Samaritan, as he traveled, came where the man was; and when he saw him, he took pity on him. He went to him and bandaged his wounds, pouring on oil and wine. Then he put the man on his own donkey, brought him to an inn and took care of him. The next day he took out two denarii and gave them to the innkeeper. 'Look after him,' he said, 'and when I return, I will reimburse you for any extra expense you may have.'

"Which of these three do you think was a neighbor to the man who fell into the hands of robbers?"

The expert in the law replied, "The one who had mercy on him."

Jesus told him, "Go and do likewise." Luke 10:33-37

All Christian institutions have quantitative ways by which they measure success. Christian schools may measure students and staff, while churches may measure “nickels and noses.” As Followers of Christ we must engage in measuring our active participation in being a biblically inspired neighbor. This will cause inconvenience and cost money. It did for the Samaritan, yet it is the Samaritan’s model Jesus commands us to emulate.

Christian institutions may attract flocks of followers and build wonderful buildings, but have they been a model of Jesus teaching? If they have not intentionally neighbored; if they have not sacrificed something for their neighbor, I am not sure the Bible allows any answer other than “No.”

Questions for Reflection

Examine your life, how good of a neighbor are you? If you need improvement, how do you feel you could be a better neighbor?

If you go to a church, answer the above questions about your church?

12 | LOVE

This book sought to tell the story of one person who took seriously the belief that God created him with intentionality and had a place for him within the Kingdom purposes for this world. The living out of such a calling has resulted in the creation of what I deem to be one of the best examples of urban ministry found in the city of Atlanta, if not in the country. Thus, this book is also the story of the Atlanta Youth Academy.

As the Bible enables me to understand it, we are all created with intentionality. God has a hope for all people within God's Kingdom purposes in this world. Ephesians proclaims "we are God's workmanship, created in Christ Jesus to do good works, which God prepared in advance for us to do" (2:10). If you do not intentionally seek to discover that Kingdom hope and purpose in your life you miss out. God does not dislike or abandon you; there is no curse in scripture that your life will be void and meaningless. God, however, has an immense amount of fullness and love that can fill even the darkest corners of each person's life.

It is this love that Larry felt as a young man who had lost his father and nearly his own life because of the reckless acts of a few wayward men. Through these dark corners of his life the evil one could have worked to kill, steal, and destroy him by propelling racism and stereotypes. God had a grander design. Larry opened himself up to experience the restorative healing of God's love, even within the most sensitive emotional, spiritual, and physical wounds. In turn, Larry has been able to express love rather than hate or indifference.

This love is not just an ethereal, feel good love. The love of God, as displayed in the Bible, is tangible and concrete. This chapter will very briefly follow the love of God, as it is understood biblically. I hope you and I will be convicted that the only response to God's love is to be intentionally on mission with God here upon this earth. You may not be called to quit your job and start a school that works with inner city children. God does, however, have a hope and a purpose for you to transform this world in your own way, within your own context, because of, not in spite of, your background.

Love as commitment to covenant.

Within the culture of the Old Testament, the most visible display of God's love was faithfulness to covenant. God made a covenant with the people of Israel, where Israel would not cease to be God's people and the people would inhabit the land of Israel.

The LORD appeared to us in the past, saying:

"I have loved you with an everlasting love;

I have drawn you with unfailing kindness.

I will build you up again,

and you, Virgin Israel, will be rebuilt.

Again you will take up your timbrels

and go out to dance with the joyful.

Again you will plant vineyards

on the hills of Sama;

the farmers will plant them

and enjoy their fruit.

There will be a day when watchmen cry out

on the hills of Ephraim,

'Come, let us go up to Zion,

to the LORD our God.'"

Jeremiah 31:3-6

By the time the prophet Jeremiah prophesied these words the people of Israel had already broken faithfulness with God. They had turned away and had been taken into captivity by Assyria and Babylon. The power of God's love was displayed not in the people's faithfulness to God, but in God's faithfulness to them. Despite the people's unfaithfulness, God never forsook the covenant, and the people never ceased to be God's people. It was because of God's love and faithfulness to covenant that the Israelites would be restored to the Promised Land.

Too often, we read a mean and angry God into the Old Testament, yet the grand narrative of the Hebrew scripture displays a God who is overly generous in love and faithfulness to a people who often lack faith. That faithfulness, however, does not come without a hope and expectation from God for the people to be faithful as well. Upon returning to Israel after exile, Ezra, the priest, and others call the people to return to their faith in God. Just as God restored the people back to the land, the religious leaders had a responsibility to help restore the people back to God.

Love as bond between God, us, and others.

By the time we arrive at the gospels, the narrative of the biblical story develops in such a way that Jesus becomes the living metaphor by which we can better understand God's love.

"As the Father has loved me, so have I loved you. Now remain in my love. If you keep my commands, you will remain in my love, just as I have kept my Father's commands and remain in his love. I have told you this so that my joy may be in you and that your joy may be complete. My command is this: Love each other as I have loved you. Greater love

has no one than this: to lay down one's life for one's friends. You are my friends if you do what I command. I no longer call you servants, because a servant does not know his master's business. Instead, I have called you friends, for everything that I learned from my Father I have made known to you. You did not choose me, but I chose you and appointed you so that you might go and bear fruit—fruit that will last—and so that whatever you ask in my name the Father will give you. This is my command: Love each other. John 15:9-17

The story of Jesus not only displays God's love for humanity but also allows a divine glimpse into how the Holy One desires us to treat one another. This is a fundamental shift, but it is not exclusive to the New Testament. The prophets of old had been calling the people of Israel to engage in mercy, justice and love with one another as an expression of their faith (i.e. Micah 6:8). Now, however, Jesus revolutionizes our understanding of faith by declaring our faithfulness to love each other as an equal expression of our faithfulness to God.

Love as ultimate expression of God's power.

The early ethos of Christianity was particularly Jewish. From her origin the church carried with it many of the Jewish traditions, rituals, and vocabulary. Jews would have had trouble understanding the "once and for all" sacrifice theology which was espoused by Jesus' early followers. Paul, writing to a diverse audience (even before the Gospel of John was penned), expresses his understanding of the love of God as a force so powerful it overcomes all.

No, in all these things we are more than conquerors through him who loved us. For I am convinced that neither death nor life, neither angels nor demons, neither the present nor the future, nor any powers, neither height nor depth, nor anything else in all creation, will be able to separate us from the love of God that is in Christ Jesus our Lord. Romans 8:37-39

The audience of *Romans* would have likely contained those who believed nothing occurred after death. Deists of all sorts would have understood Jesus as one amongst a host of divine beings. And, former Jews who were wrestling with whether sin separates them from God regardless of the actions of Christ. Here in this text, the love of God is expressed not as a part of God's character but as the ultimate expression of God's power. Paul is articulating that there is nothing within all the realms of existence more powerful than God's love.

Love as ultimate expression of the *missio dei,* mission of God.

The biblical narrative continues to develop in such a way that the love of God is not only the ultimate expression of God's power but is the ultimate expression of God's mission.

Dear friends, let us love one another, for love comes from God. Everyone who loves has been born of God and knows God. Whoever does not love does not know God, because God is love. This is how God showed his love among us: He sent his one and only Son into the world that we might live through him. This is love: not that we loved God, but that he loved us and sent his Son as an atoning sacrifice for our sins. Dear friends, since God so loved us, we also ought to love one another. No one has ever seen God; but if we love one another, God lives in us and his love is made complete in us. 1 John 4:7-12

The text communicates something very important to the Johannine audience: in loving one another, we are doing nothing less than being the very presence of God here in this world. In fact, 1 John goes as far as to say God's love is made complete when we love another. Such a comment is a powerful testimony to our participation in a love for which the letter clearly reminds us was not initiated by humanity. God loved us first—the only response to such love is to participate with God in loving others.

With love being such an ambiguous word, what is the content of this love we are to display? If we travel back to the original context of the ultimate expression of God's love in the Old Testament, we are reminded that God's love is what comforted the people in their darkest times of exile. This love then allowed them to rebuild and be restored back to God's hope for them in the land of Israel.

The times we participate most as active agents of God's love in this world are when we work alongside God to rebuild people's lives. To co-labor with Christ and restore humankind back to the God that created them with intentionality, hope and purpose in this world. This is evangelism rightly understood; this is the *Missio Dei*, the Mission of God.

Participation in and display of this kind of love takes on various forms. For Larry, it was the development of a school. For others, it may be volunteering regularly in a battered women's shelter or working to develop clean water resources in Africa. For others, it is intentionally being the presence of Christ in the business world and generously giving time, talents, and financial resources to ministries like the Atlanta Youth Academy.

What about you? I am confident that you were created with intentionality in the image of God. This God loves you and has remained faithful to you even in your darkest day. God continually seeks to rebuild and restore you into the fullness of life. Biblically, the most appropriate response to God's restorative love is to reciprocate that love to others.

Responding fully to this kind of restorative love requires moving past any cultural expectations that may limit you. Larry and nearly every child he has worked with have one thing in common: cultural expectations. Although their expectations may differ, the ability to overcome them for the sake of the Kingdom is no less important for either.

I tell this story not because Larry is a saint. He would be the first to assure you he is far from it. Larry never excelled in school. Dealing with dyslexia and ADHD, he ranked just below average in his academic pursuits. He is a normal follower of Jesus who decided to put a lot of faith in his sense of call in this world. This story is his story and his alone. The testimony of the gospel is that *you* have a story as well. May you be granted with the courage, discipline, and faith to live out your story in the world.

And may we end with paraphrased words from Paul's letter to the church at Philippi:

Finally, brothers and sisters, whatever is right, whatever is pure, whatever is lovely, whatever is admirable- if anything is excellent or praiseworthy- think about such things. Whatever you have learned from or received from this story- put into practice. And the God of peace be with you.

Philippians 4:8-9 (paraphrase)

Questions for Reflection

Describe your understanding of the love of God?

What is one thing you take from this story and how can you implement that into your life?

ABOUT THE AUTHOR

Rev. Dr. Tony Lankford

Currently the Senior Pastor of Atlanta's historic Park Avenue Baptist Church, Tony grew up just south of the city in Fayetteville, GA. He is a graduate of Shorter University (B.S.) and Mercer University (M.Div & D. Min). Tony, along with his wife and two children, reside in the Grant Park neighborhood of downtown Atlanta. He is also the author of *Living Call: An Old Church And A Young Minister Find Life Together.*

WITH THE HELP OF

Rev. Dr. Larry Teem

A husband and father of five is a native Atlantan from the Buckhead community. He is a graduate of The Lovett School, Auburn University, Immanuel Baptist Seminary (M.Div), and Urban Seminary of Atlanta (D.Min). Larry became involved in urban ministry during the summer of 1984 in Techwood Homes (the first Government housing project in the United States). He served as the first Youth Minister at Church of the Apostles Atlanta, GA.

In 1991 he founded and became President of the Atlanta Youth Project - an urban ministry providing programs and activity support for over three thousand youth & families in the metro Atlanta area. He is also the Founder and Chairman of the Board of Directors of the Atlanta Youth Academy & serves as a Trustee of The Atlanta Youth Academy Foundation. The Atlanta Youth Academy provides a Christ-center, college preparatory school grades k-4 through 8th to underprivileged youth in the inner city of Atlanta. Larry also founded and chairs the boards of Community Village, a non-profit affordable housing ministry, and Urban Seminary of Atlanta (USA), which trains and equips urban leadership.

About Chuck Johnston

Born in 1940, Chuck Johnston grew up in Atlanta's Buckhead neighborhood, attending Atlanta Public Schools that were segregated at the time both for elementary and high school. He followed his two older brothers by going off to Vanderbilt to college.

While in college he knew he wanted to teach English and coach (primarily track, which had been his sport in college). Upon graduation (1962), Chuck taught 10th grade English to all-boys classes at The McCallie School. McCallie was followed by a year in France studying and travelling, a year back at Vanderbilt for a Master's degree, and then to an education of teaching and administering at numerous school, in this order: Westminster (Atlanta), Brookstone (Columbus, GA), Berry Academy (Rome, GA),Trinity School (Atlanta), and Robert Louis Stevenson School (Pebble Beach, CA). With the interval of being the executive director of the Atlanta Ballet and president of the Children's Education Foundation, he concluded his career with schools with Whitefield Academy (Atlanta), and the Atlanta Youth Academy. While at Berry Academy, he did achieve a second masters in the inaugural class of Emory's Executive MBA program.

Now in his 70's, Chuck lives with his art-teacher wife JoElyn in the Bankhead neighborhood of Grove Park. He is president of Grove Park Renewal LLC, an effort to achieve in a long-established African-American residential community what Bob Lupton calls "gentrification with justice."

EDITORIAL HELP

Carol Hogan & Trey Lyons

Appendix

Chuck Johnston

Retiring Executive Director, Atlanta Youth Academy

How can we do what we do better?

The key to any school's success is the choice of its professional leader, the choice of its trustee's chair, and the manner in which these two work together.

In your "school plan," have those things that are non-negotiable and other things you'd like have but would be willing to concede to overwhelming oppositional opinion. In other words, "Choose your battles carefully."

The head of school, by whatever title, should begin his or her day out front at morning carpool opening car doors, greeting parents and students by name, and being available for a parent who may wish to park and ask a question or have a brief conversation.

Put a high priority on compensating teachers & staff as well as possible. Provide medical insurance and a matching retirement plan. (If the school's employees receive a sub-standard compensation package, then they are, in fact, subsidizing the true cost of that education.) Many of the employees have families with the same needs and desires as those of the school's parents & trustees.

All employees want to grow in their job skills and in their interpersonal skills:

All subscribe to the handshake pledge and its spirit:

(person's name), I will always assume the best about you.

I will not talk about you behind your back.

And, if I ever do have a problem with you, I will come directly to you.

Provide financial support for further course work for staff and teachers alike.

Elevate the professionalism of the teachers.

Praise them publicly; correct them privately.

Take non-essentials "off their plates."

Teachers will know and respect the correlation

between their attendance and academic results.

Provide substitutes so the teachers can visit other schools and study other programs.

Promote the idea that teacher attendance and passion influence student achievement as much as anything else. Love the things you teach so much that students & parents see you as a bit eccentric. (Even fake that eccentricity. It contributes to learning.)

The climate of the school cannot be "us" verses "them," adult verses students. The adults are outnumbered and will lose, and you'll never have the deep corporate culture for which you strive. Respect is the key. Students respect the adults, and the adults respect the students. Treat all students with respect.

Talk openly about racial reconciliation. Work towards a fair multiethnic representation in the administration and staff as well as within the teaching corps.

Our bodies are the temples of God. We must learn to be stewards of these temples. Therefore, we must discipline ourselves towards fitness, which includes exercise, nutrition and rest. We will teach physical skills that are basic to lifetime recreational pursuits as well as to sports. Participation in team sports is encouraged because of the multitude of life lessons learned and the heightened sense of community engendered.

Here is what I think a school should be able to say about itself: *We exist to educate the hearts and souls of young people, as well as their minds. To most effectively educate, we maintain both a challenging and a nurturing environment. Since "man's chief end is to glorify God and enjoy Him forever," then that sense of enjoyment should be inherent in this learning and growing environment. We glorify God by expanding the perceived limits of that which a young person is capable. We do all in the name of Jesus and by the power of the Holy Spirit. The school will not become a surrogate parent. Rather, the school serves as an informational resource for and a partner with the families of it students.*

The academics should be as rigorous as possible. The bar should be set high, and then each teacher must make a commitment to help the willing student reach that level.

Whatever flies under the banner of Christ, be it academics, the arts, or sports, should strive to be excellent in the true sense of the word.

Scriptures upon which to build a school:

Colossians 2:6-8 So then, just as you received Christ Jesus as Lord, continue to live your lives in him, rooted and built up in him, strengthened in the faith as you were taught, and overflowing with thankfulness. See to it that no one takes you captive through hollow and deceptive philosophy, which depends on human tradition and the elemental spiritual forces of this world rather than on Christ.

Mark 10:45 ... the Son of Man did not come to be served, but to serve ....

Philippians 2:2-3 Do nothing out of selfish ambition or vain conceit. Rather, in humility value others above yourselves, not looking to your own interests but each of you to the interests of the others.

Deuteronomy 6:5 Love the LORD your God with all your heart and with all your soul and with all your strength.

Matthew 22:37, 39 Jesus replied: "Love the Lord your God with all your heart and with all your soul and with all your mind. This is the first and greatest commandment. And the second is like it: Love your neighbor as yourself.

Jeremiah 29:11 For I know the plans I have for you," declares the LORD, "plans to prosper you and not to harm you, plans to give you hope and a future."

All learning does not occur in the four walls of the classroom. Learning also occurs by going and seeing and doing.

Materials used in the classroom are chosen from among the best available, regardless of whether the source is Christian or secular; but the guidance of the teacher through these materials is always from a strong Christian perspective. We are adverse to the stereotypical Christian school eager to slap Bible verse Band Aides on the realities of the world we live in. We want to teach students to be thinkers and to examine all possible theories and perspectives on issues logically and free of emotional opinions. We believe that all truth is God's truth which allows us to acknowledge non-Christian thoughts and ideas without fear or hesitation. Just as C.S. Lewis, Josh McDowell, and Darwin himself discovered the reality of God's presence in their own efforts to intellectually disprove Him, our students will be allowed the opportunity to see how powerful and timeless God's truth is when other philosophies are measured against the Bible. God's Word will never return void.

The Bible should be taught from the youngest to the oldest, but woe be to the teacher that makes it dull and lifeless ("Better that a millstone be tied around their necks and ....") I John 2:6 says, "Whoever claims to live in Him must walk as Jesus did." So we study the Bible to learn how to "walk as Jesus did," to learn how to walk as Joshua did, and as Queen Esther did. We learn to be a singer of songs as was David, a dreamer of dreams as was Joseph, and a visionary as was John. We internalize and personalize what God has to say to us about excellence, about male/female relationships and marriage, finances, and conflict resolution. We commit Scripture to memory, and we know Genesis to Malachi, Matthew to Revelation; more importantly, we grow to know the Author intimately – "to live in Him' and to resemble Him.

Specifically for Urban Schools Serving Children from Low-Wealth Families

As a school for children from low-income inner-city neighborhoods, we will not settle for being a "pretty good school." Rather, we are determined to take boys and girls who are culturally disadvantaged and produce fine and intelligent young men and women who go on to become significant leaders. In other words, we are here to create an extraordinary school.

By the end of the 8th grade our students will be able to write an engaging and convincing three-paragraph paper that is impeccable in its grammar and style. Writing is of utmost importance.

Reading and mathematics are no less essential and will be pursued with vigor.

45% of all black students across the nation never graduate from high school. Sexually transmitted diseases are highest among the African-American population. People of God must raise up **strong Christian leadership from within the urban youth** themselves if change and positive opportunities are going to open up for urban children.

Good manner are an important aspect of leadership. Teaching students good manners – holding the door for others, for example – is not just some kind of folderol passed down from the Victorian era. It is a way of putting another person ahead of yourself and showing consideration for that person.

I think if our graduates leave here having a heart for other people in general, and particularly the less fortunate, then they are on the way to becoming energized leaders who will come back and serve their childhood communities. That's our prayer for them.

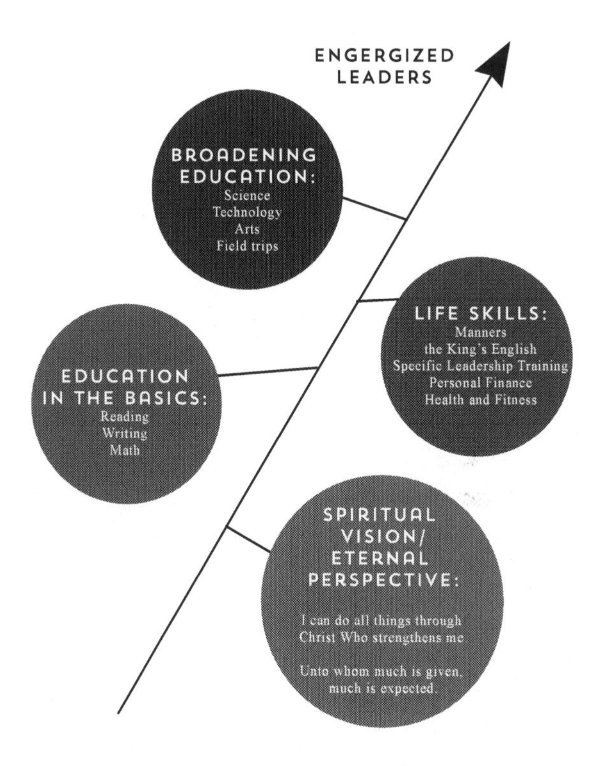

WHY WE ARE NEEDED:

"What the fish & bread meant for the thousands of hungry people standing before Christ and His disciples, a Christ-centered education means for the millions of American children who are educationally starving."
— Vernard Gant, national urban education leader

"Many urban children grow up to be unproductive citizens because they never amass the [financial, intellectual, social, spiritual] capital necessary for productivity."
Vernard Gant

In a six-year Brookings Institute study, they documented that there's a 17 times greater chance that African American children will attend a four-year college if they attend a private school.
In addition, there is a 265-point differential among African American students on the SAT if they attend private schools.

Fund Raising

My friend Allen Bell sent me a book I have liked: *Donor Centered Fund Raising*, by Penelope Burke. It has helped us see the exchange of money from a person to an institution in a new light - from the donor's perspective.

Individuals are the bed rock of our annual fund. Scholarship Partners give $12K or more to scholarship a student. Partial Scholarship Partners give between $4K and $11.9K and then over 300 additional donors give varying amounts below $4K. We treasure each gift and each donor without regard to the size of the gift. Both full and partial partners give an accumulated $900K; individuals with smaller gifts give $200K, and corporations and foundations give another $200K, giving us $1.3M as the contributed income in a $1.7M budget.

We connect a donor to a student so that the donor has a child's picture to put on the refrigerator. The donor has three occasions during the year to visit that child in his or her classroom. Ideally we have some art work or note coming from the student to the scholarship partner.

We are often asked how we sustain a school that is primarily dependent on donations. What gives us our sustainability? Organizations freely declare themselves "faith based." Our very life blood is fueled by faith. Many a season in the school's history our bank account has run thin, if not dry, and every time thus far, some unexpected sustenance has come to us, often from a source that had been unknown to us up to that point.

If we have a prospective donor on campus – always meeting students and sometimes having lunch with some – there is a high likelihood that that visitor will become a donor. Students are trained to greet strangers they see on campus by looking them in the eye, giving them a hearty handshake, and exchanging names. Each class has a greeter who rises to meet someone who visits in a class.

Notes

[i]John Claypool, God the Ingenious Alchemist: Transforming Tragedy with Blessing (Harrisburg: Morehouse Publishing, 2005), 17.

[ii]Atlanta Youth Project Newsletter

[iii]"Bridging the Achievement Between Black and White Students." online: http://www.theharrisfoundation.org/sitecontent/776/bridging-the-achievement-gap-between-black-an/category/449/the-harris-foundation-blog.aspx (accessed 15 Feb 2012).

[iv]Bob Lupton, Toxic Charity (New York: Harper One, 2011), 4-7.

[v]"Failing Reading Scores = Prison Cells." online: http://tryingtofollow.com/2006/04/10/failing-reading-scores-prison-cells/ (accessed 20 Mar 2012).

[vi]Stephen Cohen, "A $5 Book vs. a $47,000 Jail Cell- Choose One." online: http://www.forbes.com/sites/stevecohen/2010/12/25/a-5-childrens-book-vs-a-47000-jail-cell-choose-one/ (accessed 20 Mar 2012). And Manning Marable, "Incarceration vs. Education: Reproducing Racism and Poverty in America." online: http://urbanhabitat.org/node/2808 (accessed Mar 20 2012).

[vii]Bob Lupton, *Compassion, Justice, and the Christian Life: Rethinking Ministry to the Poor* (Ventura: Regal, 2007), 61.

[viii]Richard Sterns, *The Hole In Our Gospel: The Answer That Changed My Life and Might Just Change the World* (Nashville: Thomas Nelson, 2009).